OVER THE BLUE WALL

OVER THE BLUE WALL

By Etta Lane Matthews

Illustrations by James Daugherty

CHAPEL HILL · 1937
THE UNIVERSITY OF NORTH CAROLINA PRESS

Copyright, 1937, by
THE UNIVERSITY OF NORTH CAROLINA PRESS

To
the Boys and Girls
in the Land
of the Western Waters

MESSAGE TO THE READER

IN THIS BOOK I have tried to give you a picture of the "Land of the Western Waters," the land that lies between the Appalachian Mountains and the Mississippi River, when this region was the Indians' hunting ground and when the white man struggled to possess it. The explorer, after he had climbed the Blue Wall of the Appalachians, found many rivers flowing west or southwest—the Allegheny, the Monongahela, the Ohio, the Hiwassee, the Watauga, the Tennessee, and other streams large and small—all tempting him to follow them, by trail and canoe, into the heart of the continent. He heard, too, of a Great River, into which all the western waters flowed, and of riches to be found far beyond the horizon. So the "Land of the Western Waters" became a vast stage on which Indian tribes and white nations acted a great drama in many acts and scenes. Although the story takes you north, south, east and west, I have tried to tell you especially about the region south of the Ohio and east of the Mississippi.

The information has been gathered from many sources—histories, colonial records, letters that passed between the English King and the colonial governors, early travels and diaries, and biographies of the leading frontiersmen. If, through reading these pages, you have a keener appreciation of the land which is your heritage, the book will not have been written in vain.

This story would never have been begun or completed but for the aid of my friend, Mary U. Rothrock, of Knoxville, Tennessee, to whom I would have dedicated it, had I not dedicated it to you. Her aid and inspiration have really made the book possible. Others who have helped me are Ruth Hayward, who so kindly copied for me information from the documents in the Wisconsin Historical Society Library, and Nita Pyburn, of Tallahassee, Florida, who read the manuscript with great care and gave many helpful criticisms and suggestions.

E. L. M.

CONTENTS

PART I

The Spanish Search for Gold

CHAPTER	PAGE
1. THE LAND OF GOLD HATS 3	

    Ponce de León
    Pánfilo de Narvaez
    Cabeza de Vaca

2. HERNANDO DE SOTO 12
    The Lure of Gold
    The Town in the Dogwood Thicket
    America's Bloodiest Battle
    A Cruel Winter
    The Father of Waters

PART II

Frenchmen on the Great River

3. INDIAN TALES AND FRENCH ADVENTURERS   37
    Stories of the Great River
    Father Marquette and Sieur Joliet
    On the Great River

4. PRINCE OF FRENCH EXPLORERS 45
    Sieur de la Salle
    Through the Lakes to the River
    Misfortunes
    At Last the Great River
    The Man Who Got Lost
    The Journey's End

CONTENTS

PART III

The English Find the Valley

CHAPTER | PAGE
5. WESTWARD BOUND 75
   The Challenge
   Over the Blue Wall
   The Cherokee Village
   James Needham, Heroic Englishman
   Gabriel Arthur's Adventures among the Cherokees
   Home Again
   Alexander Spotswood and the Knights of the Golden Horseshoe

PART IV

Friendly Indians and Indian Enemies

6. THE CHICKASAWS 99
   The Chickasaws Obey the Great Spirit
   The French and the Chickasaws
   The Failure of D'Artaguette
   The Defeat of Bienville
   A Doubtful Peace

7. THE CHEROKEES 116
   Friends of the English
   A Visit to the Great-King-over-the-Water
   French Captives
   The Cherokee Prime Minister, Prieber
   Friends or Foes?

8. CREEK NEIGHBORS 135
   The Strongest Southern Indian Nation
   Great Mortar, Foe of the English

9. THE CHOCTAWS 145
   Allies of the French
   Red Shoes, Friend of the English

CONTENTS

PART V
Trade Rivalry and Warfare

CHAPTER   PAGE

10. VENDORS OF TRINKETS 153
    James Adair
    The Pack-train
    The Life of the Trader

11. TRADING POSTS AND FORTS 168
    The Encircling French
    The English Forts
    James Oglethorpe and the Indians
    The War of Jenkins' Ear
    George Washington Climbs the Blue Wall
    Forts for the Cherokees
    Fort-building in the Wilderness
    English Blundering
    The Siege of Fort Loudoun
    Little Carpenter, Friend of the English

PART VI
Occupying the Wilderness

12. THE HUNTERS IN THE FOREST 203
    The Life of the Hunter
    Long Hunters
    Singing in the Cane-brake
    The Giant Hunter

13. PUSHING WESTWARD 223
    Captain Bean in Watauga
    James Robertson Goes Prospecting
    Boundaries, Treaties, and Laws
    Nolichucky Jack, Indian Fighter

14. FARTHER WESTWARD 242
    The Founding of Boonesborough
    On the Cumberland
    The Voyage of the "Adventure"
    Courage in the Wilderness

CONTENTS

PART VII

The Colonies Revolt

CHAPTER | PAGE
15. THE INDIANS IN THE REVOLUTION . . . 263
   On the Warpath
   George Rogers Clark
   Nancy Ward, "Beloved Woman" of the Cherokees
   Four War Parties
   Retaliation
16. WESTERN RIFLEMEN 285
   The British in the South
   The Battle of Kings Mountain

PART VIII

The Spanish on the Border

17. SPANISH RED MEN 293
   The Spaniards and the Indians
   The Boy Who Came Back
18. SPANISH INTRIGUES 302
   Spain Holds the Great River
   Thomas Jefferson Looks beyond the Blue Wall
   INDEX 311

OVER THE BLUE WALL

Part I
THE SPANISH SEARCH FOR GOLD

I

The Land of Gold Hats

WHEN COLUMBUS with his three good ships, the "Pinta," the "Niña," and the "Santa Maria," landed on the Island of San Salvador that clear October day in 1492, he turned the attention of all Europe to a New World. Though he had not found the short route to India which he had set out to find, he had brought to the European rulers a knowledge of lands beyond the sea—a country uninhabited except by a strange race of red men and open to anyone who had the courage to explore it.

PONCE DE LEÓN

On his second voyage to America, Columbus had in his ship's company a young Spanish soldier and adventurer, Juan Ponce de León, who, a few years later, conquered the Island of Porto Rico and built on its shores the town of San Juan.

While Ponce de León was voyaging around Porto Rico and its neighboring islands, the old Indians told him of a country to the north, called Bimini, which was rich in gold. In the green forests on this Island of Bimini, they said, was a spring whose clear sparkling water made all who drank of it forever young. Ponce de León resolved some day to go in search of this island and drink from its Fountain of Youth.

Early in 1512 the King of Spain gave him permission to "proceed to discover and settle the Island of Bimini," and to be its governor, or adelantado, when he found it. Political affairs in Porto Rico kept him from starting at once, and it was not until the following year that he was able to make all his plans for the expedition which he was fitting out at his own expense.

In March, 1513, Ponce de León sailed from Porto Rico with three ships to discover the Island of Bimini and to find youth in the waters of the miraculous spring. Keeping a northward course, he first sighted the mainland of North America on March 27, Easter Sunday. Strong winds and hostile Indians made it impossible for him to land for several days. On April 2 he went ashore, a little north of the present St. Augustine, and on April 8 he took possession of the country in the name of the King of Spain. He named it Florida, from "Pascua Florida," meaning Flowery Easter, a Spanish name for the day on which he first saw the new land. From that time, all of North America was known to the Spanish as Florida and was claimed by them under that name.

Ponce de León then sailed southward around the Florida peninsula, thinking that it was an island. He explored the coast for some distance, but the shores were so damp and swampy and the Indians so unfriendly that he returned to Porto Rico. His failure to find a good landing place did not prevent him from going to Spain and telling the King and his court about the beauties of that land of flowers and asking permission to settle there. The next year (1514), through the influence of his many friends at court, Ponce de León was authorized to go and settle "the Island of Bimini and the Island of Florida," and to be its governor.

But first he was needed in Porto Rico to conquer the natives there, and this took much longer than was expected. It was not until seven years after his first attempt to find a good place to settle, that he again landed on the Florida shore. This time he was prepared to stay. He had with him priests, friars, and soldiers, with horses, cattle, sheep, and swine. But when they tried to build shelters for the colonists, the Indians tormented them constantly. Many of the men sickened and died, and Ponce de León himself was severely wounded by a poisoned arrow.

Sick and discouraged, they boarded their ships and went to Cuba. Here, shortly after, Ponce de León died from his arrow wound. He had spent all of his wealth in his King's service, and he had lost his life. He knew that he had not found the Fountain of Youth and that he had failed to start a colony in the "Island of Florida." He did not live to learn that in his search for an island he had set his feet upon a continent.

Pánfilo de Narvaez

In 1528 another fearless Spaniard, Pánfilo de Narvaez, in search of wealth and fame, landed with three hundred men and forty-two horses at a bay on the western coast of this same Florida. He named it the "Bay of the Cross"; probably it was the Tampa Bay of today.*

Narvaez left one hundred men to look after the ships, with instructions to sail along the coast to find

---

* Some students think that this was the present Apalachee Bay. It is impossible to be certain of the location of many of the places named by the Spanish explorers. The same place may first have had an Indian name, then different Spanish names, and later a French or an English name. There were no maps of the unexplored regions except those sketched by the explorers themselves. We can tell in general where they went, but exact places are not always known.

a good harbor and to wait for him there. He then started with the others to march through the country in search of the rich town of Apalache, where he had been told he would find gold and silver in abundance.

The story of Narvaez's expedition was written by one of the men who went with him, Cabeza de Vaca. This brave explorer, in his report to the King of Spain, told the story of one of the most remarkable explorations ever made on the American continent. Besides telling of the adventures of the Spaniards, he described the ways of the Indians and the plants and animals of the New World.

Narvaez at first had trouble in finding Indian guides, but finally the Spaniards met a chief who was being carried on the shoulders of an Indian. Cabeza de Vaca says that the Indian chief "wore a painted deerskin and many people followed him, and he was preceded by many players on flutes made of reeds."

The Spaniards, by means of signs, asked for guides, and the chief seemed to agree, but the Indians soon fled. Later Narvaez captured some Indians and forced them to act as guides.

Day after day they toiled through cypress swamps, waded muddy streams, crossed swift-flowing rivers, and braved the dangers of the dense dark forests. When they finally reached Apalache (probably near the present Tallahassee), they found, not a rich city, but a wretched little group of Indian huts.

After several months of hardship, discouraged, almost threadbare, and starving, they made their way again to the coast. Naturally they found no ships waiting for them, since it had been impossible for them to arrange a definite place to meet, and they had been gone so long that they had been given up for lost and the ships had returned to Cuba.

Their misfortune was complete and they hardly knew what to do. Before them lay the vast ocean, but no boats. Behind them stretched miles on miles of friendless wilderness peopled with savages all too quick with scalping knife and tomahawk. Surely it would be safer to trust themselves to the waves than to risk a horrible death in the red man's land.

Building ships was like making bricks without straw, for they had no iron, no forge, no cloth to make sails, and no tools. Their one carpenter directed the ship-building, while each man did what he could to help. Driven to desperation, they killed their horses, one a day, for food, and made water-bags of the skins. Having no use for spurs and stirrups, the soldiers beat them into axes, saws, and nails. Day and night they worked, cutting down trees with their crude axes and making planks for ships; twisting the hairs from the horses' manes and tails into ropes for the

ships' rigging, and sewing together what was left of their shirts for sails.

Late in September, 1528, they had completed five small boats. They had eaten all their horses but one. They named the harbor where they had built their boats the "Bay of the Horses," perhaps the present Ocklockonee Bay, or St. Marks Bay.

Bidding farewell to the land which had given them only misfortune, the starving and exhausted soldiers who had survived the hardships of the wilderness sailed out upon the Gulf to find their way to Mexico. Cabeza de Vaca said that the boats were so heavily loaded that they rose only six inches above the water, and the men were so crowded that they could not stir. Not one of them knew anything about the art of navigation. For ten years Spain heard nothing from Narvaez or his men.

Cabeza de Vaca

Then one day when all Seville was talking of a new expedition to Florida, a man, worn and weather-beaten, came into the King's court. Cabeza de Vaca, one of the few survivors of Narvaez's expedition, had come to ask the King to make him governor of Florida and put him in command of an expedition to that island, as North America was still thought to be. He was too late, for the commission had been given to another, but the King and all of Seville were eager to hear of his adventures.

Cabeza de Vaca told with great gusto the story of his six years' captivity among the Indians, of his escape, and of his adventures while making his way back to Spain. His travels had taken him across present-day Texas and Mexico to the Pacific Ocean. It is said that in his report to the King he gave the first description of the buffalo, which he had seen on the western plains.

In all his stories this romantic adventurer mysteriously hinted at the treasures he had seen in Florida, declaring it was the richest country in the world, that men even went to war in helmets of gold, and that they called it the land of gold hats.

2

Hernando De Soto

THE LURE OF GOLD

HERNANDO DE SOTO, who had won fame as a follower of Pizarro in the conquest of Peru, was Cabeza de Vaca's rival for the governorship of Florida. He was a bold Spanish captain and explorer who had already made several trips to America. In 1532 he had gone with Pizarro to Peru and had returned several years later with gold in such abundance that he could have lived in ease and luxury the rest of his life. When he announced his intention of leading an expedition to the land of gold hats, many men of all ranks hastened to join him.

Cabeza de Vaca's tales of misfortune and suffering were forgotten. Priests and friars, knights in glittering armor, cavaliers in silks and velvets with nodding plumes, soldiers, farmers, tradesmen, blacksmiths, carpenters—all sold everything they had for the great adventure with this man "who passed all captains and principal persons in his bravery."

No less varied than the crew were the supplies which were loaded in the ships' holds—extra armor and clothing; crucibles and sacred ornaments for celebrating the Mass; iron collars and chains for captives; forges and tools; horses, bloodhounds, and hogs—all these made up the cargo of the adventurers.

De Soto's wife, the beautiful Doña Isabel, and the wives of the principal officers went with the expedition as far as Cuba. Here De Soto left them, and, after a tour of inspection through the island, of which he was governor, set out for the mainland of Florida. On May 30, 1539, nine stately ships sailed into Tampa Bay,* on the west coast of Florida, and dropped anchor.

There are several good accounts of De Soto's travels. One of the best of them is by the "Gentleman of Elvas," who accompanied the expedition. He tells us that De Soto's first move when he went ashore was to send out a scouting party to capture Indians for guides. For a time they were unsuccessful because the Indians fled at their approach, but one day the soldiers came suddenly upon a party of ten red men, naked and hideously painted. The Spaniards were on the point of charging, and it might have gone hard with the Indians had not one of them rushed forward crying, "Do not kill me, cavalier; I am a Chris-

* Some authorities say Charlotte Harbor.

tian! Do not slay these people; they have given me my life!"

It was Juan Ortiz, one of Narvaez's men who had been captured by the Indians over ten years before and had lived among them ever since. With great joy the soldiers greeted him and took him to De Soto. By means of signs and the few Spanish words he could recall, Juan Ortiz told the story of his capture by the Indians and his life among them. The chief who captured him tied him to a scaffolding and was about to have him burned, when the chief's daughter begged the father to spare the prisoner's life, because she said it would be an honor to have a Christian for a captive. The chief agreed, and Juan Ortiz's life

was spared for the time. Later the chief's daughter warned him to flee to a neighboring tribe, where the great chief, Mocozo, befriended him.

Juan Ortiz gladly agreed to join the Spaniards as their interpreter, and the soldiers gave him clothes and armor and a fine horse.

The Spanish explorers always planned to capture Indians to act as guides and burden bearers, to grind the maize for bread, and to do the work of servants for their Spanish masters. At first De Soto had great difficulty in even finding Indians, because the forests were so dense and the land so swampy. Also the Indians had good reason to fear the Spaniards, and they warned each other by smoke signals when the

Spaniards approached. But after the soldiers had made several forays with the bloodhounds, they succeeded in catching Indians to act as guides and to carry their supplies, and the expedition was ready to set out. A strange sight it must have been—an army of over six hundred men on horseback and afoot, armed with swords, and bucklers, lances, halberds, crossbows, and arquebuses, dressed in armor or in gaily striped doublet and hose, and flowing capes; priests and friars; Indian captives in iron collars and chains, bearing on their naked backs the supplies for the expedition, and in the rear droves of clumsy hogs and a pack of savage bloodhounds.

For many weary weeks of the hot summer they toiled through forests and marshes, making their way north and west to the rich country of Apalache. Sometimes the bogs and swamps seemed impassable; always the men were harassed by the Indians. The foot soldiers were almost helpless against the nimble red warriors who darted back and forth and who could shoot three or four of their deadly arrows while a soldier was aiming once.

The cavalry did not have quite so hard a time for their horses were, to the Indians, a strange, fearful sight, but almost every day some of the horses were drowned while crossing streams or were killed by Indian arrows. By late fall, however, they were settled comfortably in the country of Apalache near the present Tallahassee, Florida, and there they stayed until early spring.

THE TOWN IN THE DOGWOOD THICKET

While they were in Apalache, Perico, an Indian guide from Mocozo's village, told De Soto of a very rich country far away to the north and east. Early in March, as soon as De Soto felt assured the cold winter was over, with Perico as guide, he directed the expedition toward this land. By this time, most of the Indians who carried the burdens had died from harsh treatment and the winter cold, for they were chained and without clothes. So the Spaniards had to carry their own grain—the cavalry, on their horses, and the infantry, on their backs. After a time they obtained more Indians for burden bearers.

After almost two months of toilsome travel, the trail they followed became dimmer and dimmer, and then faded out entirely. Perico had lost his bearings, and the knowledge that De Soto was likely at any minute to order him thrown to the dogs did not help his peace of mind. Two things, however, saved his life. Juan Ortiz declared Perico was the only Indian whose language he could understand and Friar John said that he was possessed of the devil and could not help himself.

But the army was lost in the wilderness and did not know which way to turn. De Soto sent out scouting parties to look for villages where food might be found. Then he ordered some of the precious hogs, which had been brought for just such an emergency, to be killed and half a pound of pork a day issued to the soldiers. So they gathered herbs and lived on pork and greens until one of the scouting parties brought back news of an Indian village a few miles away, where there were cribs filled with corn. Hastening to it, they ate their fill while they waited for the other scouts to join them. Then they marched together a little farther to another town called Cofitachiqui.

Cofitachiqui, which means "town in the dogwood thicket," was on the Savannah River about twenty-five miles below the present Augusta, Georgia. The Spaniards were now on the west side of the Savannah, looking across the river toward the Indian town of Cofitachiqui. Word of their coming had been sent to the woman chief, and she presently crossed the river in a canoe. Over the stern was spread an awning, under which she sat on cushions. Her chief men accompanied her in other canoes. She greeted De Soto with great dignity and graciousness, and presented him with dressed skins and shawls beautifully woven from grasses and bark. Taking from her neck a long string of pearls she threw it over De Soto's head as a token of friendship.

She then sent canoes to carry De Soto and his people across the river to the Town in the Dogwood Thicket, and supplied them with many fine turkeys and with maize and fruit. When Cofitachiqui (the princess bore the name of the village) observed that the Spanish valued the pearls very highly, she told De Soto they would find many more in the burial places of this and neighboring villages.

Following her directions, the soldiers gathered up hundreds of these gems, some of them made into figures of dolls and birds. No wonder most of the company thought this a good place to settle. The country was rich in game, fruits, and maize; and, by way of the Savannah River, ships could easily pass to and from the Spanish colonies in Cuba, Mexico, and other places. But when they urged De Soto to stop there, he replied that he was looking for a still richer country, that they could always come back if they wanted to. Since they knew he was self-willed and inflexible, they said no more.

The Princess Cofitachiqui was kind and friendly, but this did not keep De Soto from taking her away on foot, a captive, while he marched northwestward through her province. Thus the Indians could not attack De Soto's men for fear that their queen would be killed, and many of them were willing to go with De Soto to carry baggage because the Spaniards held their queen a prisoner. One day, however, Cofitachiqui and her women attendants slipped from the road into the woods. When the soldiers, missing them, turned to search, they had vanished like partridges without leaving a trace. What hurt even more than the escape of the princess was that she had taken with her a box full of the finest pearls.

"America's Bloodiest Battle"

In spite of the loss of the only treasures they had so far discovered, the Spaniards continued their northwestward march through the wilderness in search of gold. The Gentleman of Elvas says that they went to Xualla, or Qualla, through very mountainous country, and "over rough and lofty ridges" to Guaxula. This means that they crossed the southern Appalachians into the Tennessee country. Here they rested men and horses and then marched to the Tennessee River and southward to Coça, probably on the Coosa River, which they reached about the middle of July. They found it to be a pleasant land, whose plums, persimmons, grapes, and wild apples were delicious. The horses and hogs grew sleek and fat in the rich pastures of what is now Talladega County, Alabama. The soldiers rested and played dice, and,

following the savage hounds, captured Indians to take the places of those who had broken down under their loads. These they riveted together, as usual, with iron collars and chains and again took up their march.

From Coça they went southwest through Alabama to the province of Tuscaloosa. Achtahachi, the chief, was so big that the Spaniards thought him a giant. He governed a large part of what is now southern Alabama and thought himself quite as important a man as De Soto. Like a king on a throne he sat on cushions at the top of a great mound observing with a superior indifferent air while the Spaniards made their horses rear and prance before him. The Gentleman of Elvas tells us that the chief's men placed themselves around "so that an open circle was formed about him, the Indians of highest rank being nearest his person. One of them shaded him from the sun with a circular umbrella, spread wide, the size of a target, with a small stem, and having deerskin extended over cross-sticks, quartered with red and white, which at a distance made it look like taffeta, the colors were so perfect."

This great chief even kept his seat calmly when De Soto himself dismounted and came forward to greet him.

Then there were a feast and Indian dances. Altogether things went pleasantly enough till Achtahachi started to leave. To his great chagrin he discovered that De Soto had ordered him held captive. Resentful and angry, he yielded to the necessity but sent several of his chiefs on hasty errands in different directions. He pretended that this was done to get supplies for the Spaniards, but they learned to their sorrow that he had sent messengers to call together his warriors at Mauvila, or Mabile, one of his towns which lay near the head of Mobile Bay. Achtahachi promised he would give them carriers and whatever else they might ask when they reached this town.

Mauvila, they discovered, when they reached it one October morning, was situated in an open plain and was securely fenced in by a strong, high stockade. The three or four hundred Indians seemed friendly enough, many of them coming out to meet the strangers, singing and playing on reed flutes—a sign of peace. So De Soto and his men, followed by carriers with the baggage, marched inside the gates. When the dances with which the Indians always entertained their visitors began, Achtahachi quietly rose and withdrew into a house. De Soto ordered him out again, but he promptly declined to come.

Suddenly the Spaniards noticed the houses swarming with Indians. Swords flashed and arrows sang through the air. Seeing they were trapped, the soldiers dashed through the gates into the open plains. Instantly the gates slammed behind them, while the tumult of beating drums and triumphant yells filled the air. Quickly the red men struck the chains from the Indian bearers, and armed them with bows and arrows. Then they rifled the baggage of the white men, and held the spoils high above the palisades for the Spanish to see. But De Soto was too brave and determined to be routed easily. The soldiers surrounded the town, charged forward, and set it afire.

Not an Indian surrendered. Fighting like lions,

they were killed one by one till, at nightfall, only one man was left among the ruins of the town. Rather than be captured, he quickly made a loop from his bow-string and hanged himself from a limb. Hundreds of Indians perished in this bloody battle, but the Spanish too were badly wounded. All their supplies, including the pearls they had brought from Cofitachiqui, and the chalices and vestments used in the celebrating of the Mass, were burned. Eighteen or more soldiers were killed and a hundred and fifty wounded. All their medicines were destroyed by the flames; so that night they dressed their wounds with the fat cut from the slain Indians. The battle lasted nine hours and has been called the bloodiest battle ever fought on American soil.

A Cruel Winter

For a full month the Spaniards remained at Mauvila, resting and recovering from their wounds. It was then mid-November of 1540. Winter was so close on their heels that they must speedily find a food supply for the coming months of cold. Traveling north and west they came into the Chickasaw country in what is now the northern part of the state of Mississippi. They reached the little Indian village of Chickasaw in a snowstorm on the 17th of November.

They suffered cruelly from cold, for their clothing was thin and tattered, and every bit of extra cloth had been burned at Mauvila. They had had their fill of fighting and were delighted when the Chickasaw chief proposed peace and brought presents of warm deer-skins for clothing and rabbits and little dogs to eat.

They had been on the march a year and a half, but yet had found no trace of gold or silver. More than a hundred of their companions had died, either of wounds or of hardship. Others had dropped behind, sometimes to be killed or to be adopted into an Indian tribe and become savage warriors instead of Spanish gentlemen. Of those who remained, many longed to turn back southward toward the ships which would take them to safety. But the dark stern face of their commander looked steadily westward where the Indians said there was a richer land. So they lived in a palisaded village with sentries on guard at night, for they had learned to watch these tricky red men who were brave and desperate fighters.

March came with its warm winds and De Soto was eager to take the road again. They were to start early one morning. "Tonight," said De Soto the day before, when his keen eye detected a special restlessness among the Indians, "tonight is an Indian night. I shall sleep armed with my horse saddled." Unluckily, however, his cautious mood passed off and he thought no more of it, till just before daybreak when the camp broke into an uproar. It had indeed been an Indian night, for the red men, carrying coals of fire concealed in little earthen pots, had crept stealthily by the sentries and set fire to the village.

The soldiers, stopping neither for clothing nor weapons, dashed from the flames headlong into the waiting ambush. Not one would have escaped with his life had it not been for the horses. Some of these terrified animals succeeded in breaking their halters and they, too, plunged madly from the burning town. The Indians heard the flying hoofs and, thinking that mounted soldiers were charging them, turned and fled. A rain began to fall; so the red men returned no more that night.

The condition of the Spaniards was pitiable. What little clothing they had saved up to that time was burned, and many had not even had time to catch up their skin garments. They suffered from cold, and could get relief only from large fires. "They passed the night long in turning, . . . for as one side of a man would warm, the other would freeze." As soon as they could gather themselves together, they made camp a mile away, set up a forge, retempered their swords, made new saddles and crude lances from the hardwood ash trees. They wove long grasses into mats for blankets and cloaks. When the Indians came a week later, the soldiers met them bravely and put them to flight.

The Father of Waters

In spite of the loss of more than fifty horses and four hundred hogs in the Chickasaw attack, De Soto remained firm in his determination to march still farther westward, and a few weeks later, on May 8, 1541, the army stood on the bank of the biggest river they had ever seen, somewhere not far below the Chickasaw Bluffs.* They called it simply the Great River. This, had De Soto only known it, was the great discovery in the New World which was to keep his

* One writer says that the crossing was made either at Council Bend or at Walnut Bend, in Tunica County, Mississippi, from twenty-five to thirty-five miles below Memphis.

name alive; but, as he looked into the muddy swirling current, his only thought was how to get across and continue his search for gold.

Without delay he set some of his men to building shelters for the army, others to gathering corn from the neighboring villages, and still others to cutting down huge trees for rafts. Scarcely had they begun to work, when some savages came down the river in canoes and, stepping cautiously ashore, announced that their chief was coming next day to call. To be sure he did. Seated in the rear of a big barge with an awning spread over him, he floated majestically down the river to the Spanish camp. Surrounding his barge were two hundred canoes filled with warriors, standing erect from bow to stern, decorated with yellow paint and great bunches of white and many colored feathers, carrying bows and arrows and feathered shields, with which they protected the oarsmen. Three boats drew up to the bank and De Soto was presented with a great quantity of fish and dried persimmons shaped into loaves. The Spaniards watched them so closely that if they intended to attack they changed their minds when the Spaniards shot several of their number with the crossbow. Many times afterward they came and looked but did not molest the workers.

After a month's hard labor four barges were fin-

THE GREAT RIVER

ished and launched on the Great River. With horsemen and soldiers constantly on the alert, the barges carried load after load until by noon the whole army was across and "gave thanks to God," because they thought, "nothing more difficult could confront us."

Through the long summer days, De Soto and his men plodded steadily on to the north and west following the rumor of gold which, like the end of the rainbow, was always beyond. A party of explorers even went into what is now Missouri, while the main body stayed in Arkansas. But they came back and reported, as usual, no gold. When cold weather came, they marched into an Indian village and took the best part of it for themselves, building a high strong fence around their encampment. The winter was severe, but they had plenty of wood to burn; corn, beans, and dried fruit to eat; and the Indians taught them to catch rabbits in traps. They fared very well but they were saddened by the death of Juan Ortiz, their interpreter. Without him they had great difficulty in talking with the Indians and this made them feel helpless and bewildered.

With the mild weather of spring, De Soto led his weary disheartened men southward, intending to find the seacoast and thence return to Cuba for fresh men and supplies. He was determined to return and to advance still farther west.

But, in spite of his iron will, the wilderness conquered him at last. Floundering through the swamp of the Great River, he became ill with fever and, after lingering a short while, died just three years after he had sailed so eagerly to this land of Florida.

Since the Indians always had been told that De Soto was a god, the Spaniards now tried to conceal his death. They buried him secretly just inside the gate of their village where they camped. The keen eyes of the Indians, however, noticed some freshly turned clods of earth. Knowing that the Governor, as De Soto was called, had been ill and not seeing him, they became suspicious and asked Luis de Moscoso, the new leader of the Spaniards, what had become of him. Moscoso replied that he was ascended into the skies as he had often done before, taking some of his soldiers with him and that he would be there for some time. Then, fearing that the Indians might begin to investigate for themselves and find De Soto's body, the Spaniards stole out at midnight and secretly dug it up. Pouring sand into the folds of the blankets in which the body was wrapped to make it heavy, they gently placed it in a canoe and paddled noiselessly out to the middle of the river. There, under the shelter of darkness, they tenderly and reverently lowered the body of their commander into its muddy depths.

So ended the life of Hernando de Soto, the leader of one of the most famous expeditions in American history. Today, broad highways follow parts of his trail through the wilderness—that trail along which he led his strange procession of soldiers, priests, and friars; horses, bloodhounds, and hogs; Indian slaves, in chains, bent beneath the heavy burdens of their conquerors. De Soto was harsh and cruel and relentless, but his courage was very great, his spirit unbreakable. Neither the heavy heat of swamps in summer nor the bitter cold of a prairie winter could turn him from his purpose. Only death could stop him.

When his followers had buried their leader, they made their way to the Gulf. There they built small boats and followed the coast to Mexico. There were only half as many as had started out, with banners flying, on the gold-hunting expedition of the great Spaniard. After De Soto's death Spanish explorations in the land of Florida ceased, and the Indians in the valley of the westward-flowing waters lived peacefully in their villages and roamed at will through the forests, unmolested by any except other red men. For nearly a century and a half the Great River rolled down to the sea with never a white man on its turbid waters.

ROUTES of the EXPLORERS

Part II

FRENCHMEN ON THE GREAT RIVER

3
Indian Tales and French Adventurers

STORIES OF THE GREAT RIVER

IN THE CENTURY after the death of De Soto, a few Spanish settlements sprang up in Florida; the English planted little scattered villages along the Atlantic seaboard from the Carolinas to New England; and in Canada the French drove a wedge of settlements inland along the St. Lawrence River toward the Great Lakes and called the whole region New France. Except for these widely scattered colonies, the thousands of miles of forests and plains which formed the Valley of the Mississippi were still unbroken wilderness.

From the French settlements in Canada, Jesuit missionaries had gone out into the distant Indian villages, where they lived among the red men. Their main purpose was to convert the savages to the Christian faith, but these black-robed priests, who were all well educated men, did not miss an opportunity to learn about the New World. They listened closely to the stories the Indians told them of a wonderful country to the south and west which was full of game and fur-bearing animals—a country peopled with huge monsters which would devour them and with Indians who would kill and eat them. No less marvelous were the stories the savages told of a Great River that ran to the sea and was so long that many months were required to reach its mouth. All these tales the Jesuit priests wrote in the reports they sent back to France, where they were printed year after year. These reports are now known as the *Jesuit Relations*.

Members of the French court in both Old and New France read the *Jesuit Relations* diligently and carefully each year as they appeared. Boys and young men studying in the Jesuit schools pored over them and dreamed of the days when they, too, would be free to go adventuring.

Even if they did not quite believe the stories about dragons and fabulous monsters, they were curious about the Great River and the country through which it flowed. Whether it ran west to the Pacific or south to the Gulf of Mexico none could tell, for the vast plains, mountains, and deserts of the Far West as we know them were not so much as imagined by the most learned Europeans in the latter part of the seventeenth century. Some there were, however, bold enough to venture the opinion that the Great River might be the still-much-sought-after southern route to China.

Whether the river of mystery ran south or west, the beautiful, luxuriant country which it watered became a source of interest to political Old France in Paris and adventurous New France in Canada. In the latter part of the seventeenth century Colbert, the French minister in Paris, wrote to Jean Talon, the intendant, or assistant governor, of Canada: "After the increase of the colony nothing is more important for that country and for the service of His Majesty than the discovery of the passage to the South Seas."

Talon and Count Frontenac, the new governor, were given the power to select the men who were to explore this part of America and claim it for France. Fearing that the English would find their way over the mountains and take possession of the valley before the French could reach it, they chose their men speedily. Talon knew just the two for this exploratory expedition, Louis Joliet and Father Marquette.

Father Marquette and Sieur Joliet

Joliet, the son of a wagon-maker, was born in Canada and educated in the Jesuit schools there. Eight years before, Talon had heard him in debate at the

Seminary and was so impressed with his logical discussion that he had not lost sight of him. Joliet had preferred the adventurous life to that of a religious order and had left the Jesuit school to become a trader. In his wanderings among the various Indian villages he had learned the languages of several tribes; so he was well fitted for this journey into the West.

Father Jacques Marquette had been sent to Canada in 1666 by the Jesuits and had worked among the northern Indians as a missionary. Fearless, patient, and zealous for the conversion of the red men to the Christian faith, he made friends with them readily and was greatly loved and admired by them.

"Where," said Talon, "could we find two better men to go on this expedition to find the passage to the South Seas?"

So on a fair day in the spring of 1673, May 17, Joliet and Father Marquette, two loyal sons of France, with five other men, left Point St. Ignace at the Straits of Michilimackinac in two birch-bark canoes, light to paddle but strong enough to withstand the rapids which they might encounter. Their only provisions were a supply of smoked meat and Indian corn. For other food they must depend upon their guns and upon the hospitality of the Indians in the villages along the way.

Father Marquette kept a journal of their voyage,

which was preserved in the *Jesuit Relations,* and he tells us that they "joyfully" paddled westward along the northern shore of Lake Michigan and then into the waters of Green Bay. From there they entered the Fox River and dragged their canoes up its long and rough rapids until the river widened out into the quieter waters of Lake Winnebago. They crossed this lake and again entered the Fox River, paddling up-stream until they came to a short portage, which was much used by Indians and traders. Across this portage they carried their canoes, leaving behind them the northward-flowing waters, and launched the canoes in the southward-flowing Wisconsin River. Their Indian guides left them here, and the seven Frenchmen proceeded alone.

On the Great River

Down the beautiful Wisconsin River they paddled with the current, around wooded islands, past rocky cliffs, over sandy shallows, until, on June 17, they entered the Mississippi, "with a joy," said Father Marquette, "that I cannot express." They paddled southward through a beautiful country, filled with strange animals and birds. They saw buffaloes and deer and wildcats, but no Indians.

Since they were passing through country that was strange to them, they took great precautions against attack. They landed only toward evening to build small fires to cook their meals, and after eating they anchored their canoes as far out from shore as possible and slept in them. Always one member of the party acted as sentinel.

On the 25th of June they saw, at the water's edge, some footprints of men and a narrow trail leading away from the river. Thinking that it might lead to an Indian village, Father Marquette and Joliet decided to follow it. Leaving their men on guard in the canoes, they went along the little trail until they saw ahead of them an Indian village. They shouted to let the Indians know of their presence, and instantly the red men came out of their cabins. Seeing only two men and perhaps recognizing the black robe of Father Marquette, the Indians sent four old men to meet the strangers. Two of them carried calumets (long tobacco pipes of polished red stone, decorated with bright feathers), which they first raised toward the sun and then offered to the Frenchmen, in sign of peace.

Father Marquette learned that the Indians were Illinois. He and Joliet were conducted to the chief, who greeted them with the calumet, as the other Indians had done. Then Father Marquette told the listening Indians that he had come to visit peacefully the nations dwelling on the river as far as the sea.

He told them that the French wished for peace with the Indians, and he spoke of God's love for all men. Finally he asked for information about the unknown lands to which he was going.

The chief replied graciously to Father Marquette's speech, and presented him with a calumet, which would serve as a passport with the savage tribes farther south, but he begged Marquette not to go on, because of great dangers on the way.

The Indians gave a great feast of boiled corn, fish, and wild ox (buffalo). Then the white men were asked to visit the whole village of three hundred cabins. They slept that night in the chief's cabin, and the next day the chief and nearly six hundred Indians went down to the river to see them off.

Leaving the friendly Illinois, they went on southward, past the place where the Missouri River pours its muddy flood into the Mississippi, making whirlpools and currents that were dangerous to the little canoes of the Frenchmen; then still farther south, until tall canes appeared along the shores, and the Ohio came into the Mississippi from the northeast.

Wherever they landed, Father Marquette had but to hold aloft his feathered calumet of peace and the Indians greeted them as friends and brothers. They invited them to their villages and feasted them upon the best. Father Marquette and Joliet, in turn, gave them gifts of beads, hatchets, and knives, and the good priest instructed them in the Christian faith.

The chief in each village which the French visited on their journey southward told them of warlike and ferocious savages down the river and urged them to go no farther for the Indians there would surely kill them. When they reached the point where the Arkansas River runs into the Mississippi, the Arkansas Indians were so insistent upon the danger ahead of them that Father Marquette and Joliet decided they had better heed these warnings. They had traveled far enough to know that the Great River did not flow into the Pacific Ocean and so could not be the southern route to the Orient. That much was certain. It seemed wise to turn back lest they all be massacred by the hostile Indians and even this discovery be lost to France. On July 17, two months after they had started out, they turned the noses of their canoes homeward. Further exploration of the Mississippi was left to another French adventurer, who, nine years later, was to follow it to the sea.

4

Prince of French Explorers

Sieur de la Salle

WHILE JOLIET AND FATHER MARQUETTE were paddling their way down the Mississippi, a young, stalwart, dark-haired Frenchman was busily engaged in building Fort Frontenac at the outlet of Lake Ontario, and was planning a chain of trading posts from the Great Lakes to the mouth of the Mississippi. Over each post would float the white lily of France, the emblem of her power; between the posts, canoes heavily laden with bundles of furs would ply busily, and fleets of ships would carry the wealth of New France to France across the seas.

This was the great vision of René Robert-Cavelier de la Salle, who, seven years before, as a young man of twenty-three, had come to join his brother, a Sulpitian priest at Montreal. La Salle had been educated in France for the Jesuit priesthood, but his bold willful nature was not suited to the life of a priest. So he had withdrawn from the Jesuits and had come to New France, doubtless hoping that he, too, might have some part in creating a France in this country. Besides, La Salle, like all the other early explorers, was much interested in finding a passage to the Orient. Some thought that the Great Lakes would lead to China and Japan, and others believed that one of the rivers described by the Indians might be the way to the Far East.

At the time of his arrival at Montreal, in 1666, the Sulpitians, who had colonized Montreal and owned all the land around it, needed strong men to defend their town against the raids of the ferocious Iroquois. They were therefore glad to give young La Salle a tract of land not far from Montreal, upon which to establish himself. Here he built a trading post, where he exchanged guns, powder, blankets, knives, beads, and other trinkets the Indians loved, for the valuable furs so highly prized by the merchants of France. With a calm, confident manner he induced settlers to come to the new village he had laid out, and La Chine (for so it was later called, meaning China, because La Salle was so much interested in finding a way to China), became a thriving French settlement.

This location, just at the head of some dangerous rapids, was excellent as a trading center, for fur-laden canoes coming down the St. Lawrence River from the western country soon learned to stop there to rest and lighten their canoes of the heavy bundles of furs before finishing the trip to Montreal. Only a short distance north of La Chine lay the Ottawa River, another highway down which flowed a steady stream of valuable furs. Had La Salle wanted only to get rich, he could hardly have found a better spot in all New France.

But all the time that he was engaged in building and trading, he was wondering, in the back of his mind, what lay in the distant country from which the red men and the *coureurs de bois* came. He worked industriously at his fur trade and listened attentively to the stories his red visitors told him of a beautiful, flowing river which he was sure might be, or might lead to, the Great River told about in the *Jesuit Relations*, perhaps the much-sought-after route to China.

Within two or three years his property was well developed and he knew at least something of the language of half a dozen different savage tribes. When, in the winter of 1669, he explained to the Sulpitians that he wanted to give up La Chine and go exploring, they were much disturbed at what they called his frivolity, but they paid him for some of his improvements and took back part of the land. With the money he received for his land, La Salle fitted up an expedition to go into the unknown West.

With fourteen men and four canoes filled with supplies for the trip La Salle joined a missionary expedition which was going out under the direction of two Sulpitian priests. On a July day in 1669, twenty-four explorers pushed their canoes off from the La Chine shore into the placid stretch of the St. Lawrence River and headed toward the west.

Summer passed and came again and turned once more into winter and La Salle still remained in the western forests. What he did and where he went in the two years of his absence is not certainly known. It is known that about two months after leaving La Chine he parted company with the Sulpitian priests and turned south with two Shawnee Indian guides, while the rest of the party went north. He may have reached the Ohio, or Beautiful River, as the French called it, but this is doubted by many. It is known that he was looking for the Great River, which might lead to the South Seas and the way to China, and he must have made discoveries in his two years of exploring the wilderness. If he kept a journal of his travels, it has long since been lost.

When at last he returned to the French settlements on the St. Lawrence, he did not take back the news of the discovery of a new road to China, but he had caught a glimpse of the vast fertile empire of the

Mississippi Valley and realized, as never before, that the nation which controlled it, held the key to a brimming treasure chest.

In 1672, a new governor came to Canada, a bluff old lion, Count Frontenac—"Onontio, the Great Mountain," the Iroquois called him. Frontenac had not been in New France long before he realized that a trading post at the upper end of Lake Ontario would help keep the Indians at peace with the white men and would bring in from the Indians of the Great Lakes many furs which would otherwise be taken to the English and Dutch traders at Albany.

La Salle had just returned from his unsuccessful attempt to find the passage to the South Seas. He helped Frontenac make a great treaty with the Iroquois. By this treaty the French were allowed to build a trading post in their territory and the Indians promised to take all their furs to this post. Frontenac's men at once built a wooden fort, with strong palisades, which was named after the Governor, and it was in this work that La Salle was engaged when Marquette and Joliet started out on their exploration.

Frontenac decided that in all Canada none was so well suited to take charge of this important post as young La Salle, and nothing could have fitted better into La Salle's plans. The new trading post, located on the very edge of the West, offered an opportunity to build up a rich trade in furs, and to explore westward into new and unknown regions.

Though Frontenac knew La Salle was just the man he wanted, he had not the power to appoint him to the position; only the King could do that, and La Salle was an obscure young trader. Perhaps the King would want someone better known. But La Salle, who knew little of the royal court, armed with letters to influential men, and clinging to his dream, bravely set sail for France to see the King.

His proposal to King Louis was that he build a strong stone fort in place of the wooden one which had first been erected, keep a garrison there for the protection of the settlers, build a church, and pay back the money the King had already spent on the post. He would do all of this at his own expense in two years. In return, La Salle was to have the right to all the fur trade which came to the fort. The King readily agreed, and, in recognition of La Salle's services to his country, made him a member of the nobility. La Salle returned to New France with his wish granted and with a title, for henceforth he was known as Sieur de la Salle.

With boundless energy he set to work to carry out his promise to the King, and in two years he had built up at Fort Frontenac, his new post, a fur trade which brought him about five thousand dollars profit a year—a great sum in those days. But, more than ever, his eyes were fixed on that strange, fertile country—so different from the harsh frozen north —through which flowed the Great River. If only he could find it! He knew more about it now, for he had heard of the journey which Joliet and Marquette had made upon it. He was fairly certain that the river emptied its waters into the Gulf of Mexico and did not run west to the Pacific, and he saw that if France held the St. Lawrence River and the mouth of the Mississippi, she could control the great Mississippi Valley. He was equally certain that France must hasten, if she were to claim this beautiful heart of America.

Through the Lakes to the River

Though he was well on the road to wealth and independence at Frontenac, La Salle could not give up his dream of a long chain of trading posts stretching from Frontenac to the Gulf of Mexico along the banks of the Great River with settlements clustered around them. With this in mind, he again sailed to France, in the winter of 1677, to get the King's permission to explore the river and build forts along its course.

With his usual persuasive manner and bold bearing, La Salle approached the King and so impressed him with his earnestness of purpose and with the soundness of his plans that in a short time he had received the royal grant permitting him to explore and build forts in the western country, with the exclusive right to all the trade in buffalo hides for five years.

The ink was hardly dry on the royal grant before La Salle had assembled men and supplies needed for his ambitious enterprise. By July, 1678, he was on shipboard, bound for New France, with all the needed equipment—tools, rigging, and tackle for two ships he would build, one to sail the Great Lakes, the other the Mississippi: skilled workmen, shipbuilders, carpenters, blacksmiths; faithful, sturdy helpers and officers to lead them—thirty men in all.

Among the thirty was an Italian soldier, Henri de Tonty, who, in the fateful years to follow, was to prove a brave and gallant gentleman and La Salle's most loyal friend. Tonty had had the misfortune to lose a hand in a battle, and in its place he wore an iron hand covered with a glove. From this he was known as "the Man with the Iron Hand."

As soon as La Salle reached Frontenac he began to push forward his plans for the western expedition. He needed money for it, and so he sent traders to the far posts of the Upper Lakes, the Straits of Michilimackinac and Green Bay, to get furs, and he also sent men to build a fort at Niagara to control the portage path which led from the lower river around the Falls to Lake Erie. When the fort was finished, the men were to begin building one of the two ships which were a part of his plans for following the Mississippi to its mouth.

Meanwhile he and Tonty remained at Frontenac, which was the base of his whole enterprise; here they reviewed the work which had been done and made careful plans for the future. Tonty gradually learned the customs of the New World, the different kinds of furs, the trading goods, and the language of the red men. In the evening as La Salle and Tonty sat around the fires, they discussed the best routes to take, and the possible locations for the forts, and they estimated the cost.

Time passed rapidly and soon it was August of 1679. In the year since La Salle had sailed for France, everything had been placed in order at Frontenac, the Niagara post had been built, and the new ship, ready for its first voyage, rocked gently on the water. It was named the "Griffon," in honor of Governor Frontenac, whose coat-of-arms bore this symbol. It was armed with five small cannon and on its prow was a carved figure of a griffon. Safely packed aboard were the tools and supplies needed for building their second ship on the waters leading to the Mississippi.

Food, clothing, and trading goods were stowed carefully away.

The first stage of the great adventure was won, and, after a simple religious service led by the friar, Father Hennepin, the anchor was lifted and the sails spread. The ship moved forward amid the cheers of the white men and the red men's grunts of surprise and fear, for it was the first ship to sail the Great Lakes.

Misfortunes

At the end of August, 1679, they reached Point St. Ignace at the Straits of Michilimackinac (the present Strait of Mackinac), from which Father Marquette and Joliet had started out six years before. Here they stayed a few days, and La Salle found that some of the men he had sent for furs had deserted, taking with them furs and goods for trade. They were said to be at the Sault Sainte-Marie, between Lake Superior and Lake Huron, and La Salle sent Tonty to capture them and to get back his property. He himself went on to Green Bay. Here some of his traders welcomed him with a large quantity of furs. These he loaded into the "Griffon" and sent to Fort Frontenac to pay back money he had borrowed for his expedition. He directed the pilot of the ship to return with more supplies and meet him on the southeastern shore of Lake Michigan, at the mouth of the Miami River, the St. Joseph River of today.

As the "Griffon" sailed back through the lakes to Frontenac, and while Tonty was looking for the rascally traders, La Salle, with his men, made their way southward by canoe along the western shore of Lake Michigan.

His party consisted of fourteen men, in four canoes heavily loaded with a forge, tools, utensils, merchandise to trade, and arms. They carried very little food because they expected to get corn from the Indians and game by the guns of their own hunters. Among the party were three gray-clad friars, of whom Father Hennepin was one, and a Mohegan Indian hunter named Nika, who was devoted to La Salle and always went with him on his exploring trips. Tonty was to follow the eastern shore of Lake Michigan and meet La Salle at the mouth of the Miami River. The "Griffon," too, was to join them there.

But Lake Michigan was whipped by fearful storms which delayed both parties. On the first night out, La Salle's canoes barely reached the shore and were held there for several days while the gale raged on the lake. Another storm almost swamped their canoes when they attempted to land in the high breakers that lashed the western shore.

Almost starving, drenched with heavy rains, preyed upon by thieving Indians, the Frenchmen at last reached the Miami country on the first of November, but no "Griffon" rode upon the waters, and no Tonty was to be seen.

While they waited for him, they built Fort Miami (or St. Joseph), the third in the chain of forts which was to stretch from the St. Lawrence to the mouth of the Mississippi. By the time Tonty arrived, the simple fort was completed.

Still the "Griffon" did not come. Anxious to reach the country of the Illinois Indians before they should be locked in by winter ice and snow, they pushed southward, up the Miami (St. Joseph) River until they came to a portage (near the present town of South Bend, Indiana), and carried their canoes and baggage across to the Kankakee River, down which they paddled into the Illinois River. Then on they went until they came to a large village of the Illinois Indians, but they were disappointed to find it silent and deserted. The Indians had gone on their winter hunt.

A few miles farther south, where the river spreads out to form Lake Peoria, the travelers came full upon the Indians, and by skillful oratory and well chosen gifts, won their friendship.

It was now early in January, and the Frenchmen

needed rest and food. The country of the Illinois was fertile and full of game. The Indians were friendly. This, thought La Salle, would be a good place to build a fort, which could be the base of all operations in the valley. With the consent of the Indians, a fourth fort in the long chain of which he had dreamed was built and called Crèvecoeur. Scarcely was it finished before a second ship was begun, a ship which would be large and sturdy enough to sail the Mississippi and even to withstand the waves of the sea.

Winter passed and still the "Griffon" had not returned. The fear that something had happened now became a certainty. The new ship could not be finished without the equipment which the "Griffon" carried. Something must be done, and La Salle decided to return on foot to Fort Frontenac. It was now March, 1680. A thousand miles of woods and water lay between the little post in the Illinois wilderness and Fort Frontenac. La Salle knew that only strong and experienced woodsmen could stand the long overland journey, especially on the small rations that could be spared for them.

Leaving Tonty in charge of Fort Crèvecoeur and the half-built ship, he, with his faithful Mohegan hunter Nika and four picked men, set out on the long trail. For sixty-five days they tramped over frozen ground, often wading icy streams, or building rafts to get across the larger rivers, always alert to every sound lest Indian enemies surprise them. Bad news greeted them at every turn. Stopping at Fort Miami to inquire about the "Griffon," La Salle learned that the two men he had left there had heard nothing of it. At Niagara the news awaited him that the "Griffon" had utterly disappeared.

He lost no time in vain regrets. By a hasty journey to Montreal he obtained the supplies needed for the post on the Illinois. When he returned to Fort Frontenac to make final preparations for his journey back to Fort Crèvecoeur, messengers from Tonty brought news of tragic disaster.

Most of the men under Tonty had deserted, after destroying the fort and the half-built ship. Tonty of the Iron Hand was left alone and defenseless, with only two priests and three inexperienced men, and all were in danger of being attacked by the savage Iroquois, who had taken the warpath against their old enemies, the Illinois Indians. Every moment now was precious to La Salle, for the last hope of carrying out his plans lay with the brave Tonty, whom he had left at Crèvecoeur.

La Salle left Frontenac at once with twenty-four men, among them a surgeon, ship-carpenters, masons, soldiers, voyageurs, and laborers, and with supplies for a fresh start. He made all the haste he could, but three months passed before he came to the village of the Illinois Indians, only to find it wholly deserted. Where once hundreds of houses swarmed with life, now all was desolation. The Iroquois, those deadly enemies of the Illinois Indians, had scattered the stores of corn, despoiled the burial places, and set fire to the town.

The best that La Salle could hope was that Tonty and his men were captives among the Iroquois, but he determined to search relentlessly till he found some trace of them, dead or alive.

Down-stream the rescuers floated, past the ruined fort and the skeleton of the ship, watching keenly for traces of their countrymen, but finding only old campfires and terrible signs of the tortures and death which the Illinois Indians had suffered from the victorious Iroquois. When they reached the place where the Illinois River flowed into the Mississippi, La Salle gazed at last upon the river of his dreams. His men urged that they go on with the exploration; but much as he wished to do so, he refused. He must first rescue Tonty. Waiting only long enough to tie a letter for his friend to a limb overhanging the stream, he turned back toward the settlement.

This time, instead of going up the Kankakee River, when they came to the place where the Kankakee

flowed into the Illinois, they followed the northern branch of the Illinois, which led toward the western shore of Lake Michigan. They had not gone far before they saw a little deserted cabin. La Salle landed and found a piece of wood cut with a saw—sure sign of a white man—which led him to believe that Tonty had escaped from the Iroquois and was still alive.

Soon La Salle and his party left the river and went eastward overland to Fort Miami, and by the last of January they were at the fort. The following spring La Salle learned from some wandering Indians that Tonty was safe at Green Bay.

During all the time that La Salle was searching so diligently for him, Tonty himself was having serious difficulties. He and his men had at first tried desperately, though without success, to make peace between the Illinois and the Iroquois. Tonty said afterwards that there was one time when he never in all his life had been at such a loss to know what to do. While he was urging peace, one of the Iroquois chiefs stood behind him, knife in hand, and every few minutes seized him by the hair as if to scalp him. Though he felt sure they were going to kill him, he stood his ground without flinching, only hoping that when the time came they would knock him in the head instead of burning him at the stake.

Impressed by his bravery, the Iroquois gave the

Frenchmen their freedom, and Tonty and his companions lost no time in setting out for the nearest French post, Michilimackinac, at the northern end of Lake Michigan. It was winter and bitterly cold. The ground was covered with snow, and most of the time they had nothing to eat except elderberries and wild garlic which they dug out of the frozen ground. At last they reached a settlement on Green Bay, weary, ragged, and almost starved.

Spring came, and La Salle and Tonty, their desperate sufferings and anxiety behind them, joyfully met at Michilimackinac. After two years of heartbreaking work, they seemed further from success than when they started, but still they were undaunted.

Since they had no ships and few supplies, they would go in birch-bark canoes with only a small party of tried and trusty men. One thing was certain, go they would! On that they were determined.

At Last the Great River

By the fall of 1681 La Salle, with the aid of his faithful friend, Count Frontenac, had obtained supplies at Montreal for another attempt to reach the Great River. Tonty, sent on ahead, waited for him at Fort Miami, where La Salle joined him in December.

Christmas Day of 1681 found the whole party well on their way to the Illinois country. They now numbered fifty-four in all—twenty-three Frenchmen and thirty-one Indians, among whom were ten squaws and three children. They did not follow the St. Joseph River to the Kankakee, as they had before. Instead, they went in canoes to the Chicago River and followed that until they portaged to the Illinois. Since the rivers were frozen, they put their canoes and baggage on sledges and dragged them down the Illinois River until they reached open water, somewhere below the burned village of the Illinois Indians.

At the point where the Illinois River joins the Mississippi and where, the year before, La Salle had tied his letter for Tonty, they rested a week and waited, for the big stream was almost choked with floating cakes of ice which they feared would crush their frail canoes.

With the melting of the ice they resumed their journey. One day's journey down-stream, they camped for the night where the Missouri River pours its muddy waters into the Mississippi. Day after day they floated leisurely on, stopping when they chose, to fish and hunt. Passing the mouth of the Ohio, they drifted between low green banks thickly grown with willows and cane, and on February 24, they saw the high cliffs on the eastern bank now known as Second Chickasaw Bluff. This looked like promising buffalo country; so they drew ashore and the hunters promptly set out.

The Man Who Got Lost

Pierre Prudhomme, an armorer, whose duty it was to mend guns, was no hunter, but the luxuriant country tempted him to try his luck. "This time I mean to make a name for myself," he boasted as he left the camp. La Salle cautioned him not to lose his way and to watch his compass. But when evening came and the hunters returned, Prudhomme was not among them. La Salle and the others were alarmed, for they were in the country of the Chickasaw Indians. Near

by they had found a well-marked trail, which probably led to an Indian village. It was very likely, they thought, that Prudhomme had been captured.

He must be found, and in the meantime the entire party must be prepared to defend itself from attack. Then, too, thought La Salle, this high ground bordering the river was an excellent location for a permanent fort and trading post. Men set to work cutting trees and building a fort. While Tonty led a search party down the river, others roamed the woods looking for Prudhomme.

One of these groups captured two Chickasaws, whom they promptly took to their leader. Though La Salle did not understand the Chickasaw language, he treated the red captives kindly and, talking by signs, agreed to visit their village, which they told him was but two days' journey away. It proved to be much farther than that; so La Salle contented himself with sending presents to the chief and an invitation to meet the Frenchmen farther down the river. Then he turned back to his camp.

Several days later Prudhomme was found floating down the river on a raft he had made, intending to follow the canoes. Tired and starved though he was, he had made good his boast, for after this the cliffs on which he was lost were called Prudhomme Bluffs, and the fort, the first structure built by the French on the banks of the Mississippi, was named Fort Prudhomme.

The Journey's End

The misfortunes which had dogged La Salle's footsteps seemed now to have ended. All through the month of March the explorers drifted peacefully with the current through a country beautiful with spring. Buffalo, bears, deer, wild ducks, and turkeys were plentiful. They passed the place where the ill-fated De Soto had crossed the Great River over a century before. Wherever they went ashore they found the Indians friendly and generous with gifts of beans, corn, and dried fruits. Gentle Father Membré instructed the red men in religion as well as he could by sign language and rejoiced when they showed signs of understanding him. This they did by kneeling,

PRINCE OF FRENCH EXPLORERS 67

looking toward heaven, rubbing their hands carefully over their bodies after having stroked the cross.

As the explorers went farther south, they passed Indian villages and visited and talked with the tribes along the banks of the Great River. Most of these tribes were friendly, but some shot arrows at the white men. The travelers saw huge alligators and killed a number of them. They noticed the abundance of mulberry trees and thought that if silkworms were brought over from France, the Indians might be trained to make silk.

On April 6, 1682, the voyagers reached the place where the Mississippi divides into three channels. Here they separated into groups. Each group followed a channel, and three days later they met again on the Gulf of Mexico. They had reached the mouth of the Great River! All went ashore, where, in the name of the King, La Salle laid claim to the Mississippi River, all the rivers that flowed into it, and all the country drained by these rivers. Even then none knew how great was the extent of their claim.

They raised a wooden cross and a column on which were the arms of France, bearing the name of Louis the Great, King of France, and the date, April 9, 1682. Then they chanted hymns of praise and thanksgiving. A lead plate, on which were engraved the names of the explorers, was buried in the ground, and volleys were fired from the muskets. Cross, plate, and volley sealed the claim of France to the land of the westward-flowing waters, which was now named Louisiana in honor of King Louis XIV of France. Part of La Salle's dream had come true. He had followed the mysterious river to the sea, built forts, and made friends with the Indians. He had claimed the heart of America for France. But he was wise enough to see that France had yet to make her claim sure, and that she could do this only by colonists and settlements. He had yet to build and settle the little villages which he had dreamed of, clustered about the forts.

In order to make real his vision of New France in the valley, La Salle planned to plant a colony at the mouth of the river. He must hurry back to Governor Frontenac and report the success of his expedition, and then go across the waters to France and get permission to carry out his plans. Thus he would seal forever France's control of the Great Valley from the lakes to the Gulf.

The return journey was more difficult, for it was harder to pull up-stream, especially in the summer heat. La Salle, with picked canoe-men, went ahead, while Tonty with the remainder of the party followed more slowly. After a few days Tonty got a letter by way of the wilderness post-office—a limb overhanging the river. It told him that La Salle had been taken ill and asked that Jean Michel, the doctor, make all speed to Fort Prudhomme.

When Tonty himself arrived the last day of May, he found his commander desperately ill. Above all else La Salle wanted his report to go to the Governor at Quebec. So Tonty pressed forward while Father Membré stayed behind and nursed La Salle, making him as comfortable as possible in the little fort at the bluff. At last his efforts succeeded, and La Salle began to mend. After six weeks he was well enough to start again to Canada, and in September he joined Tonty at Michilimackinac.

During the following winter, he and Tonty again went down the Illinois River to the village of the Illinois and built Fort St. Louis on the great rock now known as Starved Rock. Around this fort the Illinois and Miami Indians settled, because the fort would protect them from their dreaded Iroquois enemies. All this was a part of La Salle's plan to win the Indians of the Mississippi Valley for France.

The next year, 1684, La Salle went to France and won the King's permission to take some colonists from France to settle at the mouth of the Mississippi. He set sail from France in July, with almost four hundred people in four ships, but he had many troubles. There were severe storms, and there were

quarrels among the leaders. Finally La Salle landed far beyond the mouth of the Mississippi, somewhere in the present state of Texas. He thought for a time that he was still to the east of the Mississippi, and went still farther westward looking for the Great River. He soon learned that the Mississippi was not in that direction, and turned again eastward, but he could not find it. His two remaining ships had been wrecked, so that a return along the Gulf coast was impossible.

For many weary months La Salle struggled without success to get his countrymen safely and comfortably settled. All search for the river failed. Food became scarce, and the men were quarrelsome and rebellious. At last La Salle decided to go on foot to the French settlements two thousand miles away and get help. It was while he was on this mission that one of his own men hid in the grass beside the trail and shot La Salle as he passed. He died almost instantly and was buried where he fell.

New France had lost a noble son. La Salle had not made his whole dream come true, but he had gained a strong foothold for France in America and had established a claim which in later years challenged the great powers of both England and Spain.

Part III
THE ENGLISH FIND THE VALLEY

5

Westward Bound

THE CHALLENGE

EVEN BEFORE LA SALLE had begun to dream of finding the Great River and claiming it for France, some settlers far south of Canada had become curious to know what lay beyond the lofty mountain range along their western border. For half a century the colonists in the English settlements of Virginia had gazed upon that barrier which lay between them and the unknown land beyond. Always it seemed to loom up like a vast blue wall, mocking them and daring them to venture farther.

The Indians had told them that beyond lay boundless forests filled with game, and that many days' journey away a large river flowed toward the southern seas. The English, like the French, thought this river might be the passage to the Orient, but they were more interested in the possibility of settling the country and establishing trade with the Indians there.

CHOCTAW · OC
APALACHE · SAURA
CREEK · CHERO
LOUISVILLE
MOHETAN VILLAGE
TOTERO
CHEROKEE TOWN
TENNESSEE RIVER
KNOXVILLE
CHARLOTT
SPARTANBURG
GREENVILLE
ATLANTA
AUGUSTA
COLUM
CHARLES

So, while the French were making their way down the muddy current of the Mississippi, the English were scaling the blue wall and were beginning also to claim the Great Valley. France and England, who later were to clash over the ownership of the Valley, were gradually coming closer together.

On May 17, 1673, the same spring day that Father Marquette and Louis Joliet embarked upon their expedition in search of the Great River, two Englishmen left the little village of Fort Henry, where Petersburg, Virginia, now stands. They were bound westward, but the purpose of their perilous journey was less to find the river than to discover what lay beyond the mountains.

While Joliet and Marquette prepared their canoes for the water voyage from the French mission at St. Ignace on Lake Michigan, James Needham and Gabriel Arthur made ready for an overland journey from Fort Henry. For years this fort had served as headquarters for the white traders and the red hunters from the western wilderness, and much had happened within its walls. Across the river was a village of friendly Appomattox Indians, and from it extended the great Trading Path of the Occoneechees, which led southward into rich Indian country. There was also a western trail leading over the mountains, which two Virginians, Captain Thomas Batts and Robert Fallam, had explored the year before.

Colonel Abraham Wood, the owner and commander of Fort Henry, had great hopes for the expedition which he was now sending out. James Needham, whom he had chosen as leader, was a man of education and had tramped many hundreds of miles of wilderness trails both in the Carolinas and in Virginia. Gabriel Arthur, his companion, was a strapping young fellow, keen and eager for adventure. Eight Appomattox Indians, friendly to the Virginians, were to go as hunters and guides.

The greatest danger to their expedition was the Occoneechee Island in the Roanoke River, near the Clarksville of today. This island lay southwest of Fort Henry, directly in the path leading from the white settlements to the Indian country. It was named Occoneechee Island because it was the home of a tribe of treacherous red men of that name. These Indians had been middle-men between the white traders and the distant savages so long that they did not care to give up the handsome profits of this business. They therefore did all in their power to keep the Virginians from getting in touch with the Indians to the south and west. Only a month before, they had forced Needham and Arthur to turn back.

This time, Needham hoped to prevent any such trouble by engaging one of the Occoneechees themselves to guide them into the Cherokee country—an Indian named Hasecoll, known at Fort Henry as Indian John. He was a thick-set broad-faced fellow, surly and not good to look upon. Even his own people were afraid of him.

On the day of their departure, the little village of Fort Henry was alive with excitement. Men, women, and children gathered in groups to discuss the great adventure. The friendly Appomattox Indians came from their village across the river to bid their friends farewell.

Four horses, two saddled and bridled, the others on lead halters with packs on their backs, pawed the soft earth, impatient to be off. Perhaps they, too, sensed the excitement. Finally, all good-byes said, the Indian guides took their places, Needham and Arthur swung into their saddles, Colonel Wood bade them God-speed, and they wheeled into the well-worn Occoneechee Trading Path.

Strong and fearless, Needham and Arthur had high hopes of pushing farther west than anyone had yet gone and of making friends with Indians who had never visited the English settlements. Riding along the leafy trail in the early spring was more play than work. The road was well traveled and at first they had nothing to fear. Camping at night under the open sky was an every-day matter for these experienced woodsmen. The hunters brought deer and wild turkey which they broiled over the fire. At night they planned their next day's journey. With the rising of the sun they were on their way, for they must make haste while the path was good.

When they reached Occoneechee Island, Indian John held a whispered conference with his fellow tribesmen. What was said between them no one knows. Perhaps even then Indian John was plotting against the English. At any rate, Needham and Arthur were safe for the time being, for the jealous savages had consented to let them continue their westward journey. They went happily on their way, certain now that nothing could hinder them from scaling the blue wall in the distance.

They had traveled but a short distance when they met a party of fifty-one Tomohitans, or Cherokees, as they later came to be known, coming from over the mountains to trade with the Occoneechees. Happy at being able so soon to accomplish one of the objects of the journey, Needham persuaded eleven of them to go on to Fort Henry instead of stopping, as usual, among the Occoneechees.

The forty others turned about, proudly volunteering to escort the palefaces to their village over the mountain. Indian John, if he had intended to harm the white men, had lost his chance, for the Cherokees were too much pleased with their new acquaintances to allow anyone to harm them. What the Occoneechees had feared had come to pass—the Cherokees and the white traders had met and henceforth would trade together without the aid of the middle-men.

Over the Blue Wall

On through what is now western North Carolina, past the Indian villages of Eno and Saura, the trail wound up and down and up again, growing gradually dimmer and rougher until, when they reached Sitteree, probably near the headwaters of the Yadkin River, it altogether faded out. Beyond Sitteree, white men, even the boldest of the traders, so far as was known, had never gone before.

For four days, with the Cherokees leading, they pushed their way through trackless wilds, up the rocky beds of mountain streams, burrowing like bears through tough jungles of rhododendron and laurel. They toiled through silent dense forests, up mountain sides so steep that the pack-horses could barely make the ascent.

After four days of this hard climbing, they reached the narrow crest of the Appalachians and at last they stood on the top of the great blue wall which had shut them off from the western country.

Going down was much easier than climbing up, and in another half day they had descended into what is known today as the Valley of East Tennessee. They were attracted at once by the abundance of the streams—all flowing northwestward—with great thickets of cane growing along the banks. They saw wild animals in greater numbers than they had ever seen before, and these were so tame that they scarcely seemed to notice the men as they passed. What a happy hunting ground!

The Cherokee Village

By this time they had only one of their four horses left, but a few more days of easy travel brought them to the Cherokee village. The Englishmen gazed with interest at its palisaded walls and its well-built huts. Lying upon a bluff overlooking the beautiful Tennessee River, it commanded so complete a view that only at great risk could an enemy approach by water. On the landward side the log palisades rose twelve feet high; near the top on the inside ran a narrow scaffold along which, when the town was attacked, the Cherokee warriors stationed themselves to defend it.

As Needham and Arthur looked out over the river,

they saw moored at the foot of the bluff, a hundred and fifty canoes, even the smallest of which was large enough for twenty men. Though they had been crudely hollowed out from logs, they were gracefully and slenderly shaped so that they could be handled easily and quickly in the water.

If Needham and Arthur were amazed at the completeness of their village, the Cherokees were no less surprised at their white-skinned visitors and promptly made ready to give them a great feast. Pots were set to boil and meats to sizzle. While the squaws prepared the banquet, flutes, rattles, and rolling drums called dancers from far and near to honor the guests.

Their hosts built a platform on which to display Needham and Arthur and Indian John, so that everybody could get a good look at them without jostling them. Nor was the horse forgotten. They tethered him to a stake in the center of the village and brought a feast such as he, being a horse, had never dreamed of—corn, beans, and other vegetables, trays of fish and meats and dishes of bear's oil.

JAMES NEEDHAM, HEROIC ENGLISHMAN

Now that they had found what lay over the mountains, Needham was anxious to finish his work by taking back to Fort Henry a load of furs and skins. Arthur readily agreed to remain with the Cherokees and learn more of their language and customs until Needham should return again from the fort. So Needham, Indian John, the horse, and twelve Cherokees said their good-byes and took the northward trail.

By early September they had reached home, and Needham reported their splendid success to Colonel Wood. The English at Fort Henry gave the Cherokees such a cordial welcome that they were in no hurry to return to the mountains, and it was nine days before Needham could persuade them to make the return trip with him to the village on the bluff of the Tennessee River.

Again they passed in safety through the Occoneechee village, but this time some of the evil-tempered Occoneechees joined their party. Doubtless Needham knew that this move of the jealous red men meant trouble, but he knew, too, that his only hope of safety lay in watchfulness and a bold manner. They had traveled three or four weeks and were well along the way, when Indian John became unusually surly and quarrelsome.

One evening after they had crossed the Yadkin River, as they were pitching camp near the village of Saura, Indian John scolded and growled until Needham turned to him and said, "What, John, are you minded to kill me?" Quick as a flash, before the other Indians could stop him, Indian John seized a gun and shot him dead. Then, turning to the surprised and frightened Cherokees, he told them he had been paid to do this and commanded them to go home and kill the Englishman—meaning Gabriel Arthur—in their village. Taking what he chose from Needham's pack, as much as his horse could carry, Indian John set off down the trail to the Occoneechee Island in the Roanoke River.

So died the heroic Englishman, James Needham, who had dared to climb the blue wall into the land of the westward-flowing waters.

Gabriel Arthur's Adventures Among the Cherokees

Meanwhile Gabriel Arthur was living peacefully among the far-away Cherokees, waiting for Needham's return. Little did he dream that Needham lay murdered beside the trail and that his own life was in danger. The Cherokees, who had seen Indian John shoot Needham, sped homeward over the mountain passes, uncertain all the way whether they should obey the Occoneechees and kill the Englishman or spare his life.

Unluckily for Arthur, the chief of the village was out hunting when the returning Cherokees burst in with their news. Arthur was seized and bound to a stake and a great heap of dry cane was piled about him. Hearing the cries, "Kill him, kill him," of the bloodthirsty Indians, the chief came running and reached the village just as they were about to stick the torch to the pile.

Seeing what was happening, the chief demanded angrily, "Who is he that is going to put fire to the Englishman?"

"That am I!" cried a defiant warrior, a firebrand in his hand, and almost before the words were out of his mouth, the chief had raised his gun and shot him. Then with swift strokes he cut the thongs that bound Arthur to the stake and ordered him to go to his own house saying, "Let me see who dares touch him."

Of course no one did dare touch him after that, but there were some who would have liked to kill him. The chief promised to take Arthur back to Virginia in the spring, but until then he was a captive and must live as they did, do as he was ordered, and really "be an Indian." The chief gave him a gun and a tomahawk and sent him out with a party of fifty Cherokees to raid a Spanish settlement far away in Florida. For eight days they traveled south before they came to the outskirts of a Spanish settlement. Here they skulked about the wagon road for another week before they found a chance to shoot and plunder. Then their only spoils were some gold pieces and a chain, which they took from a lone Spaniard whom they shot, and the necklace and earrings of a Negro stabbed with a piece of Arthur's broken sword.

They had no sooner reached home than another expedition was made up. This time they were to go to Port Royal, where Beaufort, South Carolina, now is, and Arthur was commanded to go along. But this was an English settlement, and Arthur refused to go, boldly telling the chief that he would rather be killed than fight against his own people. When the chief promised that they would not harm the English and that even if they met an Englishman they would let him go free, Arthur joined the party.

Setting off toward the southeast, they traveled through the wilderness for six days and came out on the headwaters of Port Royal River, where they stopped long enough to make some canoes. In these they floated rapidly down-stream till they found a convenient landing place near the English settlements, where they moored their canoes and went the rest of the way by land.

In a little more than a day they came to a house in which there were some Englishmen. Arthur and a few of the Indians crept up close to the window and listened to the voices inside. "Pox take such a master," said one, "that will not allow a servant a bite of meat to eat upon Christmas day." Not until then did Arthur know that it was Christmas, for in the Indian country no one kept track of days and months but only of seasons. As quietly as they had come, they slipped away, and the white men never knew that they had had Indian visitors that Christmas day in 1673.

At daybreak they dashed upon the Indian town they had come to attack. True enough, as Arthur had foreseen might happen, there was an English trader in one of the first houses they reached. Of course he was frightened, but he was as much surprised as frightened when Arthur called to him in English, "Run for your life!" Amazed as he was, he lost no time in running, and the Cherokees, true to their promise, let him pass through their ambush unharmed. The Indians succeeded in killing a number of their red foes and, taking as plunder the trader's knapsack full of beads, knives, and trinkets, they returned home quite well satisfied with themselves.

Next day the chief decided to pay a call on his friends, the Mohetans, who lived ten days' journey to the north in the back country of Virginia, and again Arthur was taken along. When they had made a friendly visit and were ready to start home, the chief thought he would make a three-day detour and take a whack at their old enemies, the Shawnees.

The Shawnees whacked back so hard that the Cherokees hastily retreated for, as Colonel Wood commented, "Indian valour consists most in their heels for he that can run the best is accounted the best man." Poor Arthur did not run fast enough and got an arrow wound in his thigh which stopped him completely, and so he was captured.

His captors noticed at once that his hair grew all over his head instead of being shaved with only a scalp-lock left standing, and they began to investigate more closely. They scoured him with water and ashes, and when his skin showed white they were delighted. They even gave back his gun, knife, and hatchet which they had taken when they captured him. He wanted to be as polite as they, and so he gave the Shawnee chief the knife and hatchet but told him by signs that the gun belonged to the Cherokees and he could not give it away. This suited the Shawnees perfectly, for they did not use guns much anyway.

One day when the Shawnees were cleaning a beaver to eat, Arthur noticed that they singed the fur off instead of skinning the beaver. He explained by signs that they could trade beaver-skins to the white men; four of them would buy a knife, and for eight they could get a hatchet. He suggested that they let him go back to his home and he would bring them trading goods. Pleased at this, they gave him some parched corn, put him on the trail to the Cherokee country, and let him go.

When he arrived at the Cherokee village, Arthur found them preparing for a short hunting trip which the chief wanted to make before taking him back to Fort Henry. Without resting Arthur joined the party, and they traveled almost a week, hunting and killing beaver. They seared the meat over their fires to keep it from spoiling; then, storing it in their canoes, they made their way back up-stream to the Cherokee village on the bluff by the Tennessee River.

Home Again

By this time it was May again, almost a year since Needham and Arthur had left Fort Henry on their adventure. At last the chief was ready to take Arthur back to Virginia. With eighteen of his warriors carrying packs of skins to trade, they set out along the northbound trail.

By-and-by they crossed the mountains and reached the village of Saura, where Needham had been killed. They saw, still lying scattered about on the ground, bits of goods that Indian John had thrown aside when he went through Needham's pack. Though this was a considerable distance from the Occoneechee village, the Occoneechees had not forgotten about the white man in the Cherokee country and were determined that he should not come back alive. The Cherokees found four of these crafty savages waiting at Saura.

Quite late that night when everything had quieted down and the village was sleeping soundly, these Occoneechees raised a sudden alarm that they were being attacked by a great number of strange Indians. Dazed and still half asleep, the Sauras and Cherokees took to their heels, but Arthur and one Indian boy, instead of running, hid themselves in the bushes near by. It was a bright moonlight night, and as they lay hidden Arthur could see the Occoneechees looking everywhere for him, but he made never a sound. At last they gave up the search and went home.

When they were sure the Occoneechees were gone, Arthur and his young friend lost no time in slipping out of their hiding place and setting out again for Fort Henry. Hiding by day and traveling by night they put themselves out of reach of the enemy and arrived at Fort Henry a few days later on June 18. "Praise be to God for it," wrote Colonel Wood.

While Arthur and the Indian boy were making their escape, the Cherokee chief with three of his warriors followed another and longer trail far west of the Occoneechees, and a month after Arthur's coming they, too, arrived at Fort Henry. They were cordially received, and the chief was given handsome presents for having kept Arthur under his protection. He stayed several days at the fort and when he left he promised to return "at the fall of the leaf with a party that would not be frighted by the way."

Thus the Virginians went over the mountain wall and opened trade with the western Indians.

Alexander Spotswood and the Knights of the Golden Horseshoe

About forty years after James Needham and Gabriel Arthur made their way along the Occoneechee Trading Path and over the mountains, another famous Virginia expedition started out to climb the Blue Wall. This was not a little party of traders, dressed in hunting shirts and leather leggings, following a dim Indian trail through the quiet forests, but a gorgeous cavalcade of gentlemen, guided by experienced forest rangers and Indian scouts, with a train of pack-horses laden with camping outfits, tents, large baskets of food, and plenty of wine and other beverages.

This gallant band was not going to thread its way in and out of mountain valleys, but was going to climb boldly to the top of the great Blue Wall and see what was on the other side. One writer says of Governor Spotswood that "in the mind's eye his figure will always stand on the lofty pinnacle of the

Blue Ridge, with a guiding uplifted finger pointed straight toward the Pacific Ocean and the land of infinite fertility between."

On August 20, 1714, Governor Spotswood left Williamsburg with his friend John Fontaine. The two gentlemen traveled on horseback, and when they reached Germanna, they were joined by the rest of the party—about fifty in all.

Day after day the gay company rode through the forest-clad foothills. They had abundant food, well cooked. They slept under stout tents if the weather was threatening or under the starry skies if it was clear.

On September 5, they reached the crest of the Blue Ridge and camped there for the night. The next morning they descended on the other side into the Shenandoah Valley, and Governor Spotswood buried a bottle there, containing a statement that he had taken possession of the country in the name of the King. Then they drank everybody's health, and the next day they started back to Germanna, reaching there safely at the end of three days.

Governor Spotswood had tiny golden horseshoes made, set with diamonds, and he gave one of these to each gentleman in the expedition. Because of this, the members of the party were known for many years as the "Knights of the Golden Horseshoe."

This famous expedition is only one of the things that show the interest of Governor Spotswood in the land beyond the Blue Wall. He was alert to the dangers of the settlers along the frontier and quick to respond to their calls for help. He made peace treaties with the Indians who attacked them, and did everything he could for their comfort and safety. In this way he showed his far-sighted belief that some day the land beyond the Blue Wall would be of great importance to the American colonies.

Part IV
FRIENDLY INDIANS AND INDIAN ENEMIES

6

The Chickasaws

THE FRENCH WERE NOW on the Great River, and the English had climbed the Blue Wall and were looking westward into the rich Mississippi Valley. France and England were coming closer and closer together in the New World, and soon there would be a hand-to-hand struggle. Both wanted the Indian fur trade. Both wanted the rich heart of the continent. Naturally, both wanted the friendship of the red men and were willing to do almost anything to rouse them against the white men who were enemies.

Four great Indian nations lived in the region which the French and the English were now entering: the Chickasaws, the Creeks, the Cherokees, and the Choctaws. They were often called "civilized nations," because they were more advanced than many other red men in North America.

With the French coming down from the North

and up from the South, and with the English coming in from the East, both of them seeking furs and bringing articles for trade, the Indians naturally took sides. Some of them sided with the French and some with the English. The loyalty of the Indians depended mainly upon how the traders treated them, or upon the "talks" of the governors, or upon the presents they received. A white man who lived among them once said, "Indians are but Indians, but very little to be depended upon. The highest bidder takes them off." The French "talks" were more to the liking of the Creeks and Choctaws, and even to some of the Cherokees, whose chiefs had pledged loyalty to the great King George of England, but the Chickasaws were always loyal friends of the English.

The Chickasaws Obey the Great Spirit

The home of the Chickasaws was the region near the Tennessee River in northern Alabama, extending westward to the Mississippi and southward to the land of the Choctaws.

The Chickasaw children never tired of hearing the story of how their people came from the far West into the land of the western waters. Long before our history of the valley begins, this brave and warlike tribe listened to the voice of the Great Spirit, which bade them move east into a new country, where wild game was plentiful and where there was room for many red men.

Obedient to the voice of the Spirit, the Chickasaws left their home west of the Great River and traveled eastward under the guidance of a long straight pole and the protection of a little white dog. Each night when the Indians made camp the pole was planted in the ground firm and straight, and while they slept the dog kept watch. If, when they awoke in the morning, the pole leaned toward the east, west, north, or south, they broke camp and set out on the trail in the direction which the pole indicated.

Many days and weeks they traveled, trusting themselves to the direction of the pole and the protection of the dog. After they had crossed the Mississippi River, the pole ceased to lean. Each morning the Chickasaws found it standing tall and straight. Then they knew they had reached the land which the Great Spirit meant them to have, and they started to build their villages.

Their new country lay along the eastern side of the Mississippi River, and this river became their principal highway. Indeed, they spent so much time upon it that it was called the Chickasaws' river. The high bluffs on the east bank of the river were called the

Chickasaw Bluffs, and a long trail led eastward from these bluffs to their principal villages one hundred and sixty miles away.

If La Salle had continued his journey with the Chickasaw braves that day in February, 1682, when he was in search of the lost hunter, Prudhomme, he would have found the Indians living very comfortably in well-built huts, grouped in villages which spread out over the open fields.

Each Chickasaw family had three houses—one for summer, one for winter, and one for storing corn. They were made of pine, honey-locust, or sassafras posts set upright in the ground, with the space between the logs filled with woven splits, cane, or bark. The roofs were thatched with grass or bark and were securely fastened with pegs and splits or with strips of wet buffalo skin, which shrank when they dried and were very tight and strong. Sometimes the whole was covered with clay to protect the houses from the fire arrows of their enemies. Through the open doors at each end of the summer house and through the cracks in the walls, the breezes had full sweep; but the small winter house was built so that no breath of air could get in. All cracks were filled with clay, and there was only one door, so narrow that a person could barely squeeze through, and covered with an animal skin to shut out the cold air. Even the smoke from the fire had to find its way out as best it could through a hole in the roof.

As soon as the cool days came in the fall, a fire of hickory or charcoal was built on the dirt floor in the center of the winter house, and there it burned until the warm days of spring without ever being allowed to go out. During the day the old men squatted around it parching corn and roasting chestnuts in the glowing coals while they exchanged stories about their past experiences on warpath and hunting trail.

Indian men, women, and children ate, slept, and entertained their friends in this air-tight room, which was so warm that one could sleep without covers on even the coldest nights. White traders who came to visit them in winter planned a short stay, for the hothouses sickened them and the smoke-filled air made their eyes smart.

Wooden bunks lined up against the inside walls of the house served as seats as well as beds. These were made of a framework of poles fastened to four short stakes driven in the ground. Upon this framework were placed mattresses of canes and split saplings. Blankets of buffalo and bear-skin and the furs of other wild beasts were spread over the mattresses to make the beds soft and warm. The boys slept on panther skins so that they would be brave, swift-footed, and alert, for Indian parents believed that

their children would be like the animals on whose skins they slept. The girls slept on skins of fawns and buffalo calves so that they would be modest, shy, and gentle.

Food was plentiful in the Chickasaw country, for the forests were full of game and the soil was fertile. The men were skillful hunters and the women were excellent gardeners. Beans, corn, pumpkins, and watermelons flourished under their care; blackberries, mulberries, persimmons, and strawberries grew wild in abundance. Wild turkeys fed on little red acorns and grew so fat that they could easily be run down by horses and dogs and even by the children. The country was full of beaver, but the Chickasaw hunters scorned to hunt them saying, "Anyone can kill a beaver." The chase of the swifter and more difficult game like the buffalo, elk, and deer, pleased them most.

No trail, however faint, escaped the notice of the Chickasaw warrior, and he could always tell how old it was and how many were in the party. When asked how they could do this, a Chickasaw brave replied, "White man travel with his eyes shut and mouth open. Indian travel all day, say nothing, see everything."

The Chickasaws had powerful Indian enemies; so they built strong palisades around their villages. These palisades were made of thick stakes firmly planted in the ground, and between them, in and out, were woven long splits or vines or small saplings. Then the whole was covered with clay inside and out. Loopholes were left for shooting arrows or bullets at the enemy.

The Chickasaws felt very safe in their log-palisaded villages, and well they might, for persons coming over the plains could be seen far in the distance and identified as friend or foe. If an enemy approached, the warriors quickly concealed themselves within the palisades. Then they could shoot with comparative safety through the loop-holes, and the enemy Indians found that the quiet, peaceful village was a fort from which came a deadly fire of arrows and bullets.

As the Chickasaws wandered through the valley, visiting friends and fighting enemies, they heard of the English white men who traded goods for furs. They invited the white traders to come to their villages where they, too, would give skins and furs in exchange for the English goods. Soon a well-worn trail was made leading from the English trading posts east of the mountains in the Carolinas to the Chickasaw villages. The brave Chickasaws and the English became great friends and the Chickasaws boasted that they had never harmed an English white man. No such boast could be made of their treatment of the French white men, for the French soon became the allies of their enemies, the powerful Choctaw nation which lived south of the Chickasaw country.

The French and the Chickasaws

Sixteen years after the French explorer La Salle had reached the mouth of the Mississippi, another famous Frenchman took up La Salle's work of starting a settlement there so that France could control the Great River. This was Sieur d'Iberville, who was born in Canada and who knew what it would mean to France to own the Mississippi Valley.

In September, 1698, he left France with a colony of two hundred people and abundant supplies. Some Jesuit fathers went with him as missionaries to the red men. Early in 1699 he settled his colony on Biloxi Bay, building a fort there and starting to trade with the Indians. A little later he built a fort some miles from the mouth of the Mississippi and named it New Orleans, although the present city of New Orleans was not started until 1718, by Iberville's brother, Sieur de Bienville. In 1702 a colony was settled at Mobile (Fort Louis). This, you will remember, was in the region where "America's bloodiest battle" was fought between De Soto's Spaniards and the Indians, over a hundred and fifty years before, although the Mauvila of that day was not where Mobile is today.

All these colonies and forts were planned to keep the English out of Louisiana, as the Frenchmen now called the Great Valley. With their forts on the St. Lawrence River, the Great Lakes, the Illinois River and the Mississippi River, the French planned to "encircle" the English and hold them on the Atlantic seaboard east of the Blue Wall. Iberville also tried to win all the Indians to the side of the French. In this, La Salle's old friend, Tonty of the Iron Hand, helped him, for Tonty was still trying to carry on the dead La Salle's work. From Fort St. Louis at Starved Rock on the Illinois River, he carried on the fur trade with the Illinois Indians, and kept them loyal to France. Most of the furs were now sent southward to the French settlements at the mouth of the Mississippi instead of northward to the St. Lawrence River, and so Tonty was much interested in winning the friendship of the southern Indians. Chiefly through his efforts, the Choctaws and the Chickasaws agreed to a truce, but it did not last long.

Meantime, French traders, with their packs of merchandise, tramped thousands of miles through the forests and plains of the Indian country. French boats carrying supplies, trading goods, traders, priests, and soldiers, went up and down the river between New Orleans and the Illinois country. To protect this river traffic, Bienville, in 1716, built Fort Rosalie on the spot which his brother, Iberville, had selected, near the place where Natchez now stands, and a large settlement grew up around it. In 1729 the Natchez Indians fell upon this little village and massacred most of the settlers, but two years later, the French attacked the Natchez, capturing many and selling them as slaves to the Spaniards. Those that escaped joined the Chickasaws or the Creeks.

All this time, the English were busy, too. They kept the trails hot between Charleston, in South Carolina, and the Indian country. They were skillful traders and they had better wares for trade and gave more presents than the French did. They wanted the Mississippi Valley for England as badly as Iberville, Bienville, and Tonty wanted it for France. So while the French governors made "talks" to the Indians and sent traders and Jesuit missionaries among them, the English were giving the Indians good bargains, supplying them with guns and ammunition, and doing all that they could to hold the friendship of the Chickasaws, the Cherokees, and the Creeks.

The Chickasaws traded with the French for a time, but they disliked the French and resented their making such free use of the Chickasaws' river. They did all that they could to annoy the French—captured and plundered their boats and made slaves of the boatmen and soldiers. When they learned that the French charged more for their goods than the English did, their dislike increased to bitter hatred, and they always spoke of them as "the ugly yellow French."

The French feared these cunning savages, and the Chickasaw country became a great barrier between the French settlements in the North and those in the South. Single boats could not go up or down the river safely. The traders had to go in fleets of several boats at a time and keep to the western banks of the river, watching closely all the while, with their guns ready.

At last, Bienville wrote to the King of France, "It is absolutely necessary to kill the Chickasaws if the colony is to be preserved." The King agreed to send guns, ammunition, and soldiers to help destroy the red enemy. The Natchez tribe had been wiped out. Why not the Chickasaws?

The Failure of D'Artaguette

Early in 1735 Bienville began plotting his campaign. Knowing what brave skillful warriors the Chickasaws were, he thought it best to send two armies against them, one from the south under his own leadership and one from the northern settlements under Major Pierre D'Artaguette, commander of the French soldiers in the Illinois country. Bienville offered guns, provisions, and presents to the Choctaws if they would join his army against their Chickasaw enemies, and Bienville was able to double the size of the southern army.

D'Artaguette was directed to stir up the northern Indians to go on the warpath and to bring them along with his soldiers down the Mississippi River to the Chickasaw Bluffs. They were then to march toward the Chickasaw towns and meet Bienville and his army, who were coming up the Tombigbee River, near the Chickasaw villages. It looked as if the brave Chickasaws, who had never been conquered, were at last to be overwhelmed and destroyed by these two French armies and their hundreds of red allies.

In the spring of 1735, D'Artaguette arrived at the Chickasaw Bluffs as agreed, and with the soldiers and several hundred northern Indian warriors set out for the Chickasaw country. Hearing nothing from Bienville, he sent out scouts to reconnoiter, but they returned without finding a trace of him or his army. Here indeed was a serious situation! D'Artaguette had not brought enough provisions to feed several hundred soldiers for several weeks. Besides, his Indian friends were restless and spoiling for battle. After a council of his officers it was decided that the only way to get provisions was to take them from the Chickasaws.

D'Artaguette therefore led his army against the Chickasaw villages; he was sure that it would be a surprise attack. But he reckoned without the watchful Chickasaws, who had scouts out reporting every move the French made. Just as the soldiers were starting to attack one of the outer villages, several hundred warriors suddenly came over a hill. Their terrifying war-whoop echoed over the plain. The northern Indians were frightened at this vicious onslaught and fled. The French, left to fight alone, stood their ground bravely, but they were no match for these ferocious red men, who forced them to retreat. The French provisions, guns, and ammunition were seized, and many of the soldiers, among them the gallant D'Artaguette himself, were captured and killed. Even the Jesuit priest of the French expedition was killed and the articles for performing the Mass were destroyed because the Indians thought that they were evil charms.

A Frenchman and a Negro, escaping from the battlefield, were overtaken and caught by the fleet-footed Chickasaws. Instead of keeping them as slaves or killing them, the warriors released them saying, "Live, go home and tell your people that the Chickasaw hogs have enough yellow French carcasses to last them a year. At the end of that time we would like another visit from them and their red friends."

The Defeat of Bienville

It was much less than a year, in fact less than a week, when the Chickasaws had another visit from the French and their red friends; for Bienville was even then coming up the Tombigbee River toward their villages. With seven hundred soldiers and as many Choctaw warriors, he camped within six miles of the town and sent out Indian scouts to find D'Artaguette. They reported that they had found a wide plain trail but had caught no sight of the other army. Bienville, suspecting that something had happened to D'Artaguette, decided to advance at once.

Promptly at two o'clock, with drums beating and flags fluttering in the breeze, Bienville's army marched confidently out upon the plain where lay a strongly palisaded Chickasaw village. Nearing the town, they were greatly surprised and disappointed to see the British flag floating from one of the houses. They expected to be met with a rain of arrows, but instead they were mowed down by volleys of shot from muskets. Then the French knew that rival English traders from Carolina were helping the Chickasaws defend their homes, and they did not feel so sure of winning the battle.

The Choctaws, seeing there would be no spoils of war, took to their heels and left the French to fight alone. For two hours they fought desperately, and many were killed and wounded. Bienville then saw that their situation was hopeless, and he gave the order to retreat. What was left of the French army went back down the Tombigbee River, discouraged and defeated. Not until Bienville had reached Mobile did he learn that D'Artaguette had already fought the Chickasaws and had been routed and slain. Then he knew that the powder and shot which had driven him and his men back had been captured from D'Artaguette's northern army.

A Doubtful Peace

The danger to the French colonies was now increased, for the Chickasaws, triumphant in their victory, would annoy them more than ever. Bienville was determined to lead another expedition against them, but it was three years before he could get enough men and supplies to risk another attack. This time there must be no retreating.

Again soldiers and Indians of the northern settlements and the Choctaws of the South came to his aid. To make certain this time that both armies met, he directed the northern army, under a brave French soldier, Céloron, to come in boats down the Mississippi, while he was to bring the southern army up the same river, and the forces would join at the Fourth Chickasaw Bluff. There they would build a fort to be used as a base for supplies and men. With this plan in mind, he built Fort Assumption near the present site of Memphis.

In 1739 seven hundred men arrived from France, and were transported up the river to Fort Assumption. But still there were delays. The Indian allies, always fickle, deserted and had to be won back with presents and promises. Supplies of food ran low and more had to be obtained. Illness broke out among the men at the fort. But northern Frenchmen and Indians came to help them, and at last, in March, 1740, Bienville was as ready for the attack as he ever could be. He commanded about twelve hundred Frenchmen and twenty-four hundred Indians.

He still faced a difficult task, for the streams were

swollen with heavy rains, and much of the land lying between him and the Chickasaws was under water. In the hope that war could, even yet, be avoided, he sent Céloron ahead, with a large force of men, to find out how willing the Chickasaws were to fight— or to make peace.

Meantime, we may be sure, the Chickasaws had seen all the preparations for war. They were alarmed at the numbers arrayed against them, and when the French suggested making peace, they were quite willing to do so. Bienville and his men, delighted with this peaceful victory instead of a deadly Indian battle, went back to their French settlements.

So ended the last French expedition against the Chickasaws. The French peace was not entirely successful, for the Chickasaws continued to plunder French boats and to fight Frenchmen and French Indians until the Treaty of Paris, in 1763, ended the struggle between France and England for the possession of the Great Valley, and France ceded to England all her claims east of the Mississippi River.

But the chain of friendship between the Chickasaws and their English brothers remained forever bright.

7

The Cherokees

FRIENDS OF THE ENGLISH

WHEN JAMES NEEDHAM and Gabriel Arthur scaled the Blue Wall that spring of 1673 and went down the west side of the Appalachian Mountains, they visited only one of the many Cherokee villages that were scattered through the mountainous Allegheny region. This great nation claimed many thousand square miles on the eastern border of the land of the western waters lying in the present states of Virginia, North and South Carolina, Georgia, Tennessee, and Alabama.

Legend has it that the first Cherokees came up out of a cave, for their name means "cave-people." They also called themselves Ani-yun-wiya, or "principal people." They once lived on the banks of the Ohio River, though De Soto in 1540 found them among the southern Appalachian Mountains.

Here, amid the hills, by the swift-flowing streams,

these "principal people" built their villages. They lived in three groups of towns spread out amid the hills, and the members of each group joined the others in times of danger.

A traveler on the trail from Charleston, South Carolina, to the Cherokee country would come first to the Lower Towns, which were on the southeastern side of the mountains nearest the South Carolina settlements. After another journey of a day or so, he would reach the Middle Towns, which nestled along the streams in the very heart of the mountains. Then over the hills in the beautiful valley of the Little Tennessee River, he would find the Upper, or Overhill, Towns, where lived the mountain Cherokees.

Though their towns were scattered, these red men lived as one nation, having the same friends and the same enemies. Their warriors were always fighting some neighbor. Once when the white men tried to get them to make peace with the Tuscaroras, their only reply was, "We cannot live without war. If we should make peace with them we must immediately look out for some other, with whom we can be engaged in our beloved occupation."

Though not compelled to fight, the young men were always eager to go on the warpath, for only by daring deeds could they attain the title "Great

Warrior," which was the highest honor a Cherokee could win. The days of fasting in preparation for war and drinking the "black drink" (a kind of strong tea made from the leaves of the yaupon bush), held no terrors for them, for in that way they would become virtuous, and to be virtuous was to be victorious.

Dressed in breech-cloth and scalp belt, they were ready for the trail. Starting out in single file, each walked in the tracks of the one before, the last one in line smoothing the trail so that the enemy could not tell how many were in the party, even if he found trace of them. No sound was made except an occasional signal given by imitating bird calls or the low cry of some animal.

When the Cherokees were at home they were very particular about their personal appearance. On their tattooed and painted skins they rubbed bear's oil which made their handsome stalwart bodies glisten like burnished copper. At the end of the scalp-lock, which stuck up like a bristle on their otherwise shaven heads, they tied feathers and gay-colored quills, and as a final adornment they put on bracelets, necklaces, and spangles of copper or bright-colored beads.

The Cherokee families, like the Chickasaws, each had a winter house, a summer house, and a store-house.

Every family in the village had a field where the squaws grew corn, beans, and other vegetables. Since the Cherokee horses and dogs were allowed to roam where they wished, the Indian women tried to protect their crops by fences made of stakes held together with hickory or white oak withes. When the horses would push through, as they often did, the squaws chased them out, scolding, "Go along and be sure to keep away; otherwise your hearts will hang sharp within you."

Village life among the Cherokees was not dull, for they were a sociable people and fond of outdoor sports. Ball play and chunky were their favorite games, for in them was a chance to show good sportsmanship and physical strength and skill.

Chunky was played so much that there was a special field for it called the chunky yard. The disc-shaped stone with which the game was played was highly prized and handed down from generation to generation. When the chunky stone was sent rolling over the ground, each player threw his ten-foot pole after it, aiming it so that one end of the pole would lie nearest the stone when it stopped rolling.

Ball play, a game much like our lacrosse (which the white men learned from the Canadian Indians), was often the occasion of contests between two villages or two clans. For these contests the players prepared themselves with special ceremonies, almost as if they were going to war.

Each village had a council house, where important meetings were held. With its rounded roof it looked like a small mountain, for it was built of strong timbers covered with clay, and it had no windows, and only one small door for entrance and for the escape of the smoke from the council fire in the center. Inside it was very dark and smoky. The seats were arranged in circles, one behind and above the one in front, with a clear space in the center. When a council meeting was in session, only warriors and important people were allowed to enter. They seated themselves in the rows of seats according to their rank, the greatest chiefs nearest the council fire, which was always built in the center. Those who had won the fewest honors sat at the rear. Whether the occasion of the meeting was to receive messengers of peace or to declare war, nothing was done hurriedly. Time meant nothing to them, for, they said, "The sun will rise again tomorrow."

After smoking together in silence for the better part of an hour, one chief after another would rise and make a speech. As soon as all had had a chance to give a "talk," a feast was held. Shallow baskets loaded with venison, bear, buffalo meat, and a great variety of vegetables, were passed to the guests, who ate as well as they could in the dark and without knives and forks. After the banquet all danced until morning.

Some writers called this council house the town-house, but there was another kind of town-house which was really four houses built in a square, so that they enclosed a space where many informal gatherings were held. Unlike the council house, anyone could go to the town-house, and strangers were often entertained there. The houses were open on the side of the square and were supplied with wide benches or beds along the rear, covered with mats or skins, where people could sit or even sleep at night if they wished. The other Indians of the region usually had this same type of town-house.

A Visit to the Great-King-over-the-Water

Distances meant nothing to the Cherokees, a hundred miles to them being scarcely more than a mile. They took long journeys, using the rivers as their main highways. There was nothing to keep them at home, for they could get their food as they went along—fish from the rivers and game in the woods.

But the longest trip they ever took was far away from their rivers and trails—across the water to see

the Great Father, King George. In the year 1730, a Scotsman, Sir Alexander Cuming, was led by a dream which his wife had, to visit the Cherokees. After a short visit to the Cherokee towns, Sir Alexander invited some of the principal warriors to return to England with him to see the "great man on the other side of the water."

The reason for this visit was to impress the Indians with the great power and magnificence of the English King and his court, so that the red men would be loyal to England and would not listen to the French traders and agents who were constantly trying to win them away from the English.

The Cherokee warriors were at first a bit doubtful about going so far away into a strange land, but

Eleazar Wiggan, an English trader, called by the Cherokees "Old Rabbit," who had acted as an interpreter for Sir Alexander, knew a bright young Cherokee brave named Ouconecau, who lived in his town. He was hardly more than a boy, but Old Rabbit thought he might be persuaded to take the long journey. The white men found this young Cherokee, and talked with him far into the night. At last they got him to promise to visit the Great King. When it became known the next morning that Ouconecau was going, five others promptly agreed to go, and later still another warrior joined the party.

The Cherokees stayed in England four months and were royally entertained. Wearing their native costumes, they were presented to the King, who gave them a hundred guineas and fitted them out in silks and satins like courtiers. They had a state dinner with him in Windsor Castle. Their portraits were painted as they stood under the trees in a London park. Banquets were given in their honor, and they were distinguished guests at theaters, band concerts, and fairs. For a time they were lodged at the Mermaid Tavern, where great crowds of people came to see them, until the landlord asked to have the red men taken away because they caused so much disturbance.

As the time drew near for them to return home, a great ceremony was held in which they pledged their loyalty to the King by laying at his feet the Crown of the Cherokee Nation and presenting five eagle tails and four scalps of their enemies. "The Great King George's enemies shall be our enemies," they declared. "His people and ours shall be always one and shall die together."

After a short speech, Ketagustah, as spokesman for the Indians, ended by laying the feathers upon the table and saying, "This is our way of talking, which is the same thing to us as your letters in the book are to you; and to you, beloved man, we deliver these feathers in confirmation of all that we have said." It is said that on this occasion, the Indians were painted with spots of red, blue, and green and wore only aprons of skins about their waists, with horses' tails hanging down behind.

The Cherokee warriors left the splendor of the English court and returned to their mountain home, where they lived much as before, but the young Ouconecau, who was later known as "Little Carpenter," never forgot the greatness and power of the English people, and many years later, when trouble came, he remembered his promise "to keep the chain of friendship bright as long as the rivers shall run and the sun give light."

French Captives

The Tennessee River was the principal highway of the Cherokees, and they often left their mountain homes and went in canoes down the Tennessee into the Ohio River and from there into the Mississippi, so that they might annoy the French as they passed on their way to and from their trading posts. Hiding in ambush, they captured French boats, taking the ammunition and provisions and sometimes the Frenchmen themselves.

In the fall of 1741, shortly after Bienville had made a poor peace with the Chickasaws, eighty Cherokees captured Antoine Bonnefoy and three of his companions who were on their way from New Orleans to the Illinois country. After dividing the French supplies among themselves and securing their prisoners by slave collars, the Cherokees started homeward in their twenty-two canoes. They traveled leisurely up the river, hunting and resting, and it was cold weather before they reached the Overhill villages, Chatuga and Great Tellico.

When they reached the villages a big celebration was held and the captives were the center of attraction. They were given white sticks and rattles and were ordered to sing. Not until they had sung French and Indian songs for three hours and more were they permitted to join in the feasting. Even then their trials were not over, for the next morning, bound together and dragging their slave collars behind them, they were marched to another village and taken to the town-house where each had to sing four songs. After this performance their slave collars were struck off and they were free to go and come as they pleased so long as they did not try to escape; but even this they did after some months of captivity.

The Cherokee Prime Minister, Prieber

While Bonnefoy and his companions, released from their bondage, were thinking over their affairs, a strange little man came up, and, addressing them in the most polished French, assured them he was sorry for their misfortune and offered a plan of escape. He had every appearance of an Indian but introduced himself as Pierre Albert. His real name, however, was Christian Gottlieb Prieber, and he was a German, well educated and an excellent talker. Prieber believed that this world would be a happier place to live in if all lands and crops were public property; even the children should belong to the public and be brought up and educated by the government.

He had come to Great Tellico, the principal town of the Overhill Cherokees, from Charleston, South Carolina, and the Cherokees were greatly impressed with his proposal of a new form of government with Moytoy, their chief, as Emperor and with himself as "principal secretary of state to his imperial majesty, the Cherokee chief or king." By adopting their mode of living—trimming his hair, painting his body, and going without clothes—he had endeared himself to his red friends. He taught them to weigh and measure the goods they took in trade, and he tried to persuade them to trade equally with the French and English. Because of his interest in the Cherokees and their trade, the English suspected him of being a French agent sent to win the friendship of the Cherokees and so they watched him closely.

While Prieber was living in the Cherokee village, Great Tellico, James Adair, an English trader, was living among the Chickasaws. Adair and Prieber were both interested in Indian languages and carried on quite a correspondence. Prieber got so many letters that the Indians became suspicious and asked him what "the marked large paper meant." Prieber replied that the man who made the marks was the devil's clerk and that he marked on the paper the bad speech of the evil one of darkness; whereupon they forbade him having any more to do with the devil's clerk. Adair believed firmly that Prieber was an agent of the French.

English traders in Great Tellico, who had been suspicious of him for some time, had sent reports of his doings to the government. One day Prieber wrote a letter to the officers in Charleston and signed it the "Prime Minister." The officers at once sent Ludovick Grant, a trader living in Great Tellico, to capture Prieber and bring him to Charleston. Grant knew that he could do nothing without the help of the Indians, and so he offered Moytoy, the Emperor, a great present if he would order his people to seize the Frenchman. This Moytoy would not do, for it was against the principles of the nation to give up any person who had taken shelter in their country.

But Grant had to obey his orders; so he went to the town-house alone but with very little hope of accomplishing his task. When he got there Prieber, who had learned of his scheme, merely laughed at him. Grant, angry at this, left the village and reported his failure to the government in Charleston.

Lieutenant Fox, who was then sent up with some troopers, had no better success. Failing to lure Prieber out of the village, he laid hold of him in the town-house, which was the worst thing he could have done, for it was against all Indian rules of etiquette to quarrel in the town-house. The Cherokees, who really were fond of Prieber, were exceedingly angry and told Lieutenant Fox that the country was theirs and they could do as they pleased in it. Since this was his first offense, however, they told him he would be forgiven, but he must leave their country at once. Prieber gave Lieutenant Fox a passport of safety and some of his own guards to conduct him part of the way.

When he had been in the Cherokee country about four years, Prieber set out for the French fort, Toulouse, in what is now Alabama. Landing at Tallapoosa Town in the Upper Creek country, he was captured by some English traders, who took him to Frederica, Georgia, where he was imprisoned. Out of respect for his brilliancy and education, he was given a separate room and was allowed to keep his books and writing materials and to have visitors whenever he wished. He was quite content in his prison and did not let anything worry him.

One day the fort's supply of gunpowder and bombs caught fire and there was great danger that it would explode and kill everybody in the barracks. The guards rushed about unlocking the prison doors and calling to the prisoners to shift for themselves. Prieber shifted for himself by remaining in his room only twenty yards from the burning storeroom. When all was over, the guards went to his room to see if he was there. When they had called several times, Prieber stuck his head out from beneath his feather bed and remarked, "Gentlemen, I suppose all's over. For my part I reasoned thus: the bombs will rise perpendicularly and if the fuse fails, fall again in the same direction, but the splinters will fly off horizontally, therefore with this trusty covering I thought I had better stand the storm here than hazard a knock on the pate by going further."

Prieber was kept in the barracks at Frederica until his death. Though the English always suspected him of being a French agent, he told an acquaintance that his designs in the Cherokee country were nothing more nor less than to form a great empire among the southern Indians.

Friends or Foes?

In the Cherokee country there was much coming and going of enemy Indians. Old Hop, who lived in the Cherokee town of Chota, said they were like snakes lying on the river banks ready to devour them. Some of the Cherokee warriors were even deceived by the French "talks" and offers of presents.

Great Tellico was one of the most important of the Cherokee towns, and the French thought that if they could get a foothold there they might get the entire nation away from the English. So they sent message after message to the head men to come visit them at Fort Toulouse or at Mobile. They would tell them the English were trying to drive them from their homes.

Even those Cherokees who were the best friends of the English listened to so many French "talks" that they became suspicious, and Little Carpenter—the Ouconecau who had gone to England—sometimes found it difficult not to doubt the English.

Mankiller, of Great Tellico, was the most troublesome Cherokee in the French interest. He was such a fickle, deceitful rogue that even his own family hated him and his French friends mistrusted him. For a time he had no friends in his own nation or in Great Tellico, his own town. When asked why he hated the English, he said that Elliott, a trader, had charged him too much for the goods he bought from him, and then had thrown them at him as if he were a dog out of doors.

In spite of his sulky disposition, Mankiller was a very sensitive fellow. When the head warriors of the Cherokee towns began to make fun of his loyalty to the French and when his own family turned against him, he began to wish he had never seen a Frenchman. Finally he could endure the hatred and ridicule no longer. So he promised to go with the English and help them against the French.

There were at this time other Cherokees who were suspected of being French allies. Old Hop, of Chota, who called himself the staunch friend of the English, was under suspicion because he had living at his home a white man called French John, a Canadian. He was a crafty person and had much influence over the Indians, especially over a French Indian, Savannah Tom. When Old Hop was questioned concerning this enemy in his house, he claimed that French John was his slave and he had to take care of him as a child.

With French John and Savannah Tom at Chota in close friendship with Mankiller at Great Tellico, the English had every reason to fear that the Indians of that town would allow the French to settle among them. Fortunately for the English, there were enough friendly warriors in the other towns to help them rid themselves of these enemies.

When Mankiller agreed to join the English, their next concern was French John. Once they had got rid of him, Savannah Tom would soon follow. An offer of five hundred-weight of leather was made to the Indian or Indians who would deliver French John up to the English officers. Before anyone could get to Chota to seize him, French John had run away.

About the same time that French John was living with Old Hop, another Frenchman, Chevalier de Lantagnac, was living as a trader with the Cherokees, licensed by the government of South Carolina. Lantagnac had come to the Cherokee country when he was fourteen years old. While serving as a junior officer in the French army at Fort Toulouse he had gone hunting and had got lost. After tramping several days in the woods, living upon roots and herbs, he was found by a band of Chickasaws. Feeling sorry for him because of his youth, they fed him and made him comfortable even though he did belong to the "ugly, yellow French" whom they hated. Later they gave him to the English in South Carolina.

Through the friendship that grew between him and the governor, Lantagnac succeeded in getting a trader's license. While he traded with the Cherokees he studied their manner of living and got to know the chiefs and warriors, their villages and trading paths. When the right time came, he turned over all of his valuable information to the French government.

The English believed it was Lantagnac who managed the French affairs in the Cherokee nation and that it was he who directed the actions of French John, Savannah Tom, and Mankiller in trying to win over Great Tellico to the French interest. In this he did not succeed, but, with the information he gave the French, he was the main actor in a later tragedy in the country—one which threatened the English colonies in the Carolinas and Virginia.

So intertwined and closely woven were the actions of the French Indians and the French themselves in this section of the Valley, that no one could know who were directly responsible for the evil work. As Old Hop said, they were like snakes lying on the river banks ready to devour the English and their allies.

8

Creek Neighbors

THE STRONGEST SOUTHERN INDIAN NATION

CLOSE NEIGHBORS TO THE CHICKASAWS and the Cherokees were the Creeks. Some say that they were so named because many of their villages were on the upper Ocmulgee River, which the English called Ochese Creek. The Indians were first called the Ochese Creek Indians, and this was later shortened to Creek Indians. Others say that their name was given to them because their country contained so many small streams or creeks. They were divided into two large divisions known as Upper Creeks and Lower Creeks.

The Upper Creeks lived in the hilly sections of Alabama and Georgia. They had adopted into their villages smaller Indian tribes which were fast dying out because of war and disease, until they had made themselves the strongest of the southern Indian nations. They considered themselves so superior to the

Cherokees that in one war with them, it is said, they sent only their women and boys into the fight.

The Upper Creek towns, like those of the Cherokees, were built in groups, or villages, by streams where the soil was fertile and fishing was good. The distance between their towns was so great that only on very unusual occasions did they attend the townhouse meetings of one another, so that there was not a strong spirit of loyalty among them. In fact, they had been known to be at war among themselves.

In journeying from the towns of the Upper Creeks, which were along the Coosa and Tallapoosa rivers, to the Lower Creek towns on the Chattahoochie River, one went through "red towns" and "white towns." The "red towns" were ruled over by warriors, and in them all war ceremonials were held; but the "white towns" were peace towns. In them no blood could be shed, not even that of an enemy taken in war.

In the Upper Creek villages the homes were built around the public buildings in the center. Here stood the great council house, or rotunda, and the townhouse. The great council house was usually built upon a large mound and was a huge dome or pyramid, strongly built of wood and often covered with clay like the council house of the Cherokees. It had only one opening, a door, which admitted some light and allowed the smoke from the council fire to escape. Around the sides were a series of steps or platforms for reclining, covered with woven mats or skins. No woman was allowed to enter on pain of severe punishment or death.

The town-house was really four houses built in the form of a square, which enclosed the public square, and all large public meetings were held here. The houses around the square were a good deal like those of the Cherokees. The inside was open to the square, and along the walls were broad seats covered with mats. The town-house was open to everyone.

The chunky ground was near the public square. Here young men and old men gathered for their sports and ball play. In the center of this playground was planted a tall pole upon which the Indians kept a marker as a target for arrow-shooting so that they could keep up their marksmanship.

It is said that the Lower Creeks, who lived farther south than the Upper Creeks, did not have as good houses or public buildings as the Upper Creeks, perhaps because the warm climate made them unnecessary. An early traveler among them, William Bartram, said, "They have neither the Chunky-Yard nor Rotunda, and the public square is an imperfect one, having but two or three houses . . . Their private habitations consist generally of two buildings: one a

large oblong house, which serves for a cook room, eating-house, and lodging-rooms, in three apartments under one roof; the other not quite so large . . . two stories high, of the same construction, and serving the same purpose with the granary or provision house of the Upper Creeks."

The Creek boys were taught early to endure hardships and privation. From their infancy they had to swim in the coldest weather, and on their approach to manhood, between the ages of fifteen and seventeen, they had to go through periods of fasting. Until they had been successful in battle, their position in the home was hardly more than that of a servant.

When they became warriors, the Creek men did

not neglect their homes. No party went on the warpath until the public fields and gardens had been planted. Because of their consideration for their women and children, the Creeks were said to be better homemakers than the other Indians of the "civilized nations."

But Indian women of all tribes did much heavy work. The travelers who went among the southeastern Indians in the early days and wrote descriptions of what they saw, give very different pictures of the life of the Indian women. It is certain that the women did all the work of the house. They made the pottery and wove the baskets. They prepared the skins and made clothing. They worked in the gardens and raised the corn and other vegetables. They ground the corn into meal and did all the cooking. The men hunted and fished and brought home the game. They went on war parties and engaged in ball play and chunky contests. They built the larger buildings, such as the town-houses, the council houses, the homes, and the store-houses. They felled the trees for their dug-out canoes. In the spring they usually helped the women to plant the crops in the public fields. But in the fall and winter, when they were away on their hunting trips, the women had to do everything.

One traveler says that the Creek warriors were very kind to their women. Another says that the men made slaves of the women. One says, "A stranger going into the country must feel distressed, when he sees . . . women bringing in huge burdens of wood on their backs, or bent under the scorching sun, at hard labor in the field; while the indolent, robust young men are riding about, or stretched at ease . . . amusing themselves with a pipe or a whistle."

Probably the women took their hard labor for granted, and felt that the work was evenly divided if the men did the hunting and fighting and protected the tribe from their enemies. Certainly men, women, and children enjoyed the times of feasting and games, and some of the women won high honor among their people.

Great Mortar, Foe of the English

Living, as they did, surrounded by three European nations (the French, the English, and the Spanish), and three Indian nations (the Chickasaws, the Choctaws, and the Cherokees), the Creeks learned to be very politic and crafty. From the French forts south of them came French officers to give them "talks." From the east along the trading path from Charleston came the English. On the southeast, the Spanish still laid claim to their lands and their allegiance, but did very little trading among them. The contest for their favor was mainly between the French

and the English. Each nation tried to buy their allegiance with presents. The Creeks were fully aware of the power of their position, and for some time they would not take sides with either the French or the English, preferring to trade with both.

When the French in 1717 finally built Fort Toulouse, which they had been planning for several years, near the junction of the Coosa and Tallapoosa rivers, the Upper Creeks transferred their trade to the French. Though they remained friendly to the English for a time, they were known to the English traders as French Creeks. The warriors of the Middle and Lower Towns continued to trade with the English and were known as English Creeks.

Having won over the Upper Creeks, the French sent officers from time to time to the English Creeks to invite them to the French fort. There they gave them presents and told them the English were going to take away their lands and make slaves of them. Between the visits of the English traders and the French officers, the red men were kept busy listening to their own head warriors talk about the faults or the virtues of the French and the English.

Great Mortar, a head warrior of the Upper Creeks known to his people as Yah-Yah-Tustanage, was on the side of the French most of the time. At a council meeting with the Cherokees at which he was present, the English refused to smoke the pipe of peace with him because he had been a French Creek. From that time the French found him a ready ally and had no difficulty in getting him to carry out their schemes for attacking the English traders. He, with his friends, Handsome Fellow and Gun Merchant, was very influential in the Creek towns.

The English, however, had one friend in the Upper Creek towns, Wolf King, also a great warrior. Though he was opposed in this friendship by nearly all the head men in his nation he never failed to give the English his protection when they needed it. Sometimes this was very difficult, for Gun Merchant and Great Mortar had so many more men than he had.

On one occasion the French persuaded Great Mortar to send his warriors against the English in one of the Upper Creek towns. During the skirmish some of the traders escaped and ran to Wolf King for protection. Wolf King had only a few warriors and could not go out and help them fight, but he gave them guns and ammunition and led them to a thick swamp near by. From this vantage point the traders fought off the warriors of Great Mortar, who had followed them. Supplied with food by Wolf King, they made their way to the next friendly town under the protection of Wolf King's own men. There they met other traders and went with them to Savannah Town.

The French Creeks not only annoyed the English in their own nation but were continually going to and fro in the Cherokee country to stir up trouble. In these schemes Great Mortar was often the leader. Through him the French attempted to supply the Cherokees with gunpowder, bullets, and knives in efforts to win their friendship. Had it not been for the English Chickasaws, one of the French plots would have succeeded in wiping out all the English colonies. Great Mortar had made his home on the northern Georgia border, where he could send out scalping parties and annoy the colonists until they were forced to leave their cabins. They might have done much more harm, but, as Adair says, "our friendly gallant Chickasaws, being well informed of the ill design of this nest of hornets, broke it up." They marched against Great Mortar's settlement. Great Mortar was driven from his stronghold, many of his warriors were killed, among them his brother, and he withdrew into his own nation. There are some who think that he and his remaining warriors later joined the lawless bands of Chickamaugas which were so troublesome during and after the American Revolution.

9

The Choctaws

Allies of the French

WHEN DE SOTO, two hundred years before, forced the chief, Achtahachi, to join his march in the land of gold hats, he brought upon himself the enmity of one of the strongest and most treacherous Indian nations, for Achtahachi was a Choctaw chieftain.

Adair, the English trader who lived among the Chickasaws, said that the Choctaws were the most artful ambuscaders and wolfish savages in America, as well as the most deceitful and ungrateful. He said, too, that they had "a surprising flow of smooth artful language" and were such skillful thieves that they could steal things from under a man's very nose while he was talking to them. They were closely related to the Creeks but were also their bitter enemies.

They were sometimes called "Flatheads," because of their flattened heads, which they thought beautiful. When the babies were born, the Choctaw mothers tied bags of sand on their foreheads and kept them there until the weight had shaped the child's head to the desired flatness. One traveler described it this way: "They [the mothers] use a roll [bag of sand], which is placed upon the babe's forehead, it being laid on its back on a flat board, and swaddled [wrapped] down hard thereon, from one end of this engine [board] to the other. This method makes the child's body and limbs as straight as an Arrow. . . . The instrument I spoke of before, being a sort of a press . . . in which they make the child's head flat. It makes the eyes stand a prodigious way asunder; the hair hangs over the forehead like the eaves of a house, which seems very frightful." He went on to say that the reason the Indians did this was that it made the sight stronger so that they could see game a long way off, and thus become good hunters.

The Choctaw towns were in the middle and western part of what is now Mississippi, south of the Chickasaws and west of the Creeks. It was a fertile, rolling country, with many small streams but few large rivers. The towns were not built on an organized plan as were those of the Creeks and Cherokees. The towns along the border of the Creek and Chickasaw countries were built with the houses close together and arranged for defense, but in the towns in the center and along the Mississippi, the houses were widely scattered, for the Choctaws were a more agricultural people than were the neighboring tribes. It was said of them that a stranger might be in the middle of one of their largest communities without seeing more than half a dozen houses.

Accustomed to a level country, they became swift runners and were skilled in chunky and ball play, their chief sports, but in the art of swimming they were no match for their Creek neighbors. Having so few rivers in their country, they had not learned to swim. This was a great handicap, especially in the Creek country, where often a river or creek was their only way of escape. The Creeks ridiculed them and said they were like wolf cubs who would not take to the water but to the thick swamp as their place of safety against the enemy.

Being such a treacherous and deceitful people, the Choctaws were always on the alert for enemies and were excellent fighters as long as they fought in their own country. In the enemy's country they lost courage, and the best warrior was the one who could run the fastest. The chief concern of the warriors before they went on the warpath seemed to be how they would look when they were dead. They would ask the traders for new blankets and shirts "that they might make a genteel appearance in English cloth when they died."

Though their ancestors had resented Spanish intrusion when De Soto captured their chief two hundred years before, the Choctaws were not hostile to the French voyageurs who traded in their nation. There were more French Indians in their towns than in those of any other southern Indian nation, and they often joined the French in their campaigns against the Natchez and Chickasaw Indians.

The French did not trust them, however, for they seldom let them have more than from five to seven guns in a town. When the owner of a gun had hunted for one moon, or month, he rented his gun to another Choctaw for a moon. The Choctaw braves were excellent marksmen and were considered the best deer killers in the country.

Red Shoes, Friend of the English

The French themselves, while they held the allegiance of the Choctaws, were partly responsible for the split in the nation, forcing a part of them to the English side. Red Shoes, a much respected warrior, was loyal to the French until a French trader mistreated his wife. Red Shoes then withdrew at once from the French interest and invited the English to bring their trade to his town. As long as he lived, he protected the English traders in his own country and on their way to and from the Chickasaw towns.

Though his own people hated him for his loyalty to the English, they did not dare molest him or his friends, for he was an influential chieftain in spite of his English allegiance.

One day while he was escorting an English trader from the Chickasaw towns he fell ill. One of his own countrymen offered to take care of him on the homeward trail, and all would have gone well if this young man had not been tempted by a French reward for the death of Red Shoes. Unable to resist the French presents, the youth shot and killed Red Shoes while he lay resting.

The French were very politic in dealing with the Choctaws. They always treated them courteously and appealed to their conceit and vanity by giving them medals and presents and by appointing them to offices with high-sounding titles. In this way they managed to keep the friendship of most of them. Only a few sided with the English, and even after France had ceded her possessions to Great Britain the French Choctaws remained hostile to the colonies.

Part V
TRADE RIVALRY AND WARFARE

10

Vendors of Trinkets

AFTER THE FEARLESS EXPLORERS who had found the way into the Great Valley came the traders, with their packs of the white man's goods. Knives, hatchets, and guns, bright-colored cloth, beads, and mirrors, which the white man had been giving to win the friendship of the Indians, now became "money" to buy the furs and skins which were so plentiful in this new land. Thus a gainful trade was built up between the white men and their red neighbors.

Down the Mississippi floated the fur-laden canoes of the French. The trail that was blazed into the Cherokee country by James Needham and Gabriel Arthur, at the cost of Needham's life, was much traveled, and the trails from Charleston and other English settlements along the coast to the Indian villages over the mountains were worn deep by the traders' pack-trains. Along the southeastern edge of the Great Valley, the Spanish, in their scattered Florida settlements, bargained with the Creeks and other Indians who came their way.

The land of the western waters was a vast expanse of unsettled country, but it was not big enough for three European nations. The rivalry in the fur trade in the Valley grew more and more bitter until it broke out into open warfare in 1756, during the French and Indian War.

But we may forget for a time this bitter rivalry and think of the lives of the fur traders who for years lived and worked among the Indians and knew them better than any other white men, except perhaps the missionaries. These traders loved the life of trail and camp, the ever-present spice of danger. It is hard to find stories more interesting than the lives of the early fur traders.

Using the rivers and streams as their highways, the French traders wandered through the Valley, bargaining here and there with Natchez, Chickasaw, and Choctaw Indians and with whatever Creeks and Cherokees they could persuade to buy their wares. When the French goods—cloth, knives, guns, and hatchets—had been traded for the skins of beaver, deer, and other wild animals, they made their way with their furs down the rivers to the French trading posts of Mobile and New Orleans.

Ordinarily the French stayed in the Valley and in the Indian villages just long enough to close their deals with the Indians, but as early as 1710 a Frenchman whose name we do not know built a trading post at French Lick, where Nashville, Tennessee, now stands. He lived there with a fourteen-year-old boy called Charleville. Charleville later bought out the Frenchman and carried on the trade himself, living in the Indian country until he was an old man.

The Indians whose villages were near the English settlements carried their furs upon their backs to the white trading posts, but those who lived at a great distance, like the Overhill Cherokees, did their business with traders who carried their goods on packhorses into the Indian towns and there exchanged them for the pelts which they took to the settlements.

One of the first traders to live with the Indians in their towns was Cornelius Dogherty, an Irishman. In 1690, when he was just a young man, he went from his home in Virginia to the Cherokee towns, where he lived and traded until, it is said, he was nearly one hundred and twenty years old.

James Adair

While Dogherty was living with the Cherokees, James Adair, one of the bravest of the early traders in the Great Valley, made his home in the Chickasaw country. For forty years he lived among them "like a friend and brother" and was often called the "English Chickasaw."

Adair was not only a trader but a prosperous farmer and a scholar as well. His home in the Indian village was like a small plantation, with horses, chickens, and turkeys feeding in the fields. In his gardens could be found most of the fruits and vegetables that grew in the Chickasaw country. While his Indian wife took care of his household, he spent his spare time in writing down his impressions of the Indians and all he could learn about their country, customs, and language. His book, *The History of the American Indians,* is now an important source of information about the Indians in the southeastern United States.

The trader's store-house was full of never-ending interest to the Indians, from the smallest child to the greatest warrior. There were guns, powder and bullets, hatchets and knives for the men when in hunting mood. For their holiday times, there were beads, mirrors, clothing, paint, and gaudy jewelry, for even the warriors were very vain. In fact, a young redskin did not think himself properly dressed unless he had a looking-glass slung by a leather strap over his shoulder. The squaws wanted ribbons, red and blue stockings, needles, scissors, thimbles, and hoes. For the little girls there were dolls which the traders called "double-jointed babies."

If a squaw or a warrior wanted a red belt it could be bought cheaply—for only a few skins, but salt, gunpowder, teakettles, and looking-glasses were in such demand that no price was set. The traders got as much as they could. The skins which were used as money might be raccoon, otter, mink, muskrat, beaver, elk, deer, and buffalo.

During the winter months the traders lived in the Indian villages while the red hunters and trappers went into the forests and camped for weeks at a time killing their game and dressing the skins. When spring came and they had enough skins to return to the settlements, the traders from the different villages loaded their horses and set off in one long caravan for the eastern settlements. In the autumn, or, as the Indians said, "at the fall of the leaf," the pack-horses were loaded again, this time with English goods, and the traders returned to the Indian country.

The Pack-train

Twice a year, spring and fall, the forests echoed with the shouts of the caravan drivers and the tinkling of the horse-bells. Little animals scampered from the path, and the larger ones hid themselves in the thickets, watching, perhaps, for a chance to attack the caravan as it made its way through the wilderness.

If the previous season had been prosperous, the westward moving pack-train might have as many as one hundred horses, with fifteen or sixteen traders and pack-horse men to keep them in line. Fifty of the horses would be loaded with packs weighing about one hundred and fifty pounds each. When these horses became tired from the long hard journey, the packs were shifted to the backs of the fifty fresh horses which had been following at a leisurely pace. Even the best horses could make only twenty miles a day in the hilly country, and if a caravan were going to the Chickasaw country, it would be on the road six weeks; while the shortest journey from the English settlements to the near-by Cherokee towns took ten days.

Sometimes young colts which had never been broken were used. It required a great deal of tact and patience on the part of the pack-horse man to load them, for of course they would not stand still while the packs were being strapped on. When the driver had tried everything else, he would tie the restless colt to a post and then take the tip of its ear between his teeth and bite it hard. One bite was usually enough to curb the young creature, and it would stand quietly until loaded.

When all packs were in place and the horses were lined up in Indian file, oldest first and youngest last, the chief driver took his place at the head of the line. Assured that all was ready, he gave one loud crack of his long leather whip, whooped, and shouted the command to start. Each driver in turn, with the crack of his whip, passed the signal on, and the pack-train started on its way. As the horses trotted briskly along, the grass or leaves which had been stuffed in their bells joggled out, and a merry tinkle added music to the caravan. Up hill and down the horses trotted until they were too tired to go any farther. Then, even though it might be only mid-afternoon, the caravan stopped and camped for the night.

The wilderness trails were hard going, for they

led through dense forests and along paths which were unbroken except where bear and buffalo had pushed their way through the underbrush. Up rugged mountain sides, along narrow ledges, down rocky ravines, the daring trader guided the pack-train, always alert to the cracking of a twig or the moving of a bough which might warn him of a hidden enemy—a silent crouching panther, a deadly rattler, or perhaps an enemy red man.

Often the trail would lead to the edge of a stream and lose itself along its rocky floor, and some way had to be found for the caravan to cross and pick up the trail on the other side. If the stream was narrow, a raccoon bridge could be quickly made, for it was only necessary to cut down a tree which was long enough to reach to the other side. Upon this the men crossed, while the horses waded the stream.

In order to cross a deep wide stream a raft had to be made, and that took time and work. Trees eight or nine inches in diameter were cut down, the branches trimmed, and the trunks cut into nine-foot lengths. Twelve or more of these trunks were placed on the ground side by side and securely bound together with tough vines. On top of this foundation were placed bundles of dry canes and timber to make a floor upon which to load the packs and protect them from the water. To each end of the raft was fastened a vine long enough to reach across the river. When the packs had been taken from the horses and loaded on the raft, a pack-horse man who was a good swimmer would take the end of one of the vines and swim across drawing the raft after him. On the shore the raft was unloaded and pulled back by his companions on the opposite bank. Back and forth the raft was pulled by its tow-line until all the train—packs and traders—were over, while the horses, without their packs, swam across. Again the horses were loaded and the caravan resumed its trail.

As the pack-train neared an Indian village, the drivers gave their call and cracked their whips to announce their arrival. Indian chiefs and warriors marched out to meet them and escorted them in, for the traders were considered important people, and the arrival of the white men with their goods was a holiday occasion.

The Indians always expected presents, particularly rum, or "fire-water," as they called it. This the traders were not allowed to give them, for when the Indians got drunk they were very quarrelsome and certain to get into trouble. Sometimes they would hang around and beg so persistently that they were a great nuisance.

One day Adair had tried in vain to get rid of a young Choctaw who wanted fire-water. At last he took a bottle of pepper-sauce and laid it on the table, explaining that he used it only when he ate and then only a very little. Seizing the bottle, the greedy Indian gulped down a quantity of the fiery liquid. Gasping and stroking his throat, he shared his bottle with a thirsty friend until together they had drunk it all. By this time the pepper-sauce burned so that all the water they could drink was not enough to cool them off, and Adair was never bothered again with their begging for rum.

The Life of the Trader

When a trader had won the firm friendship of the Indian chief and his warriors, he was allowed to choose the site for his home. He might build it in the center of the village where he would be protected from skirmishing parties of Indian enemies, or, if he preferred, he could live on the edge of town, where he had more space for his garden, poultry, cattle, hogs, and horses. His livestock would be as safe on the outskirts as they would be in town, for the young Indians were almost as destructive to the pigs and poultry as were the wolves and foxes.

Wherever it was, the trader's house was usually the largest and best in the village and stood out "like a tower in the city." In addition to his own living quarters, he had a store-house for his goods and furs, and a winter house, such as the Indians used, for the women and children of his household. With an abundant supply of meats, nuts, and fruits from the forest, vegetables from his own garden, and sugar, tea, and other delicacies from the white settlements, the trader with his Indian wife often lived as comfortably and happily as his friends and relatives in the English colonies.

As soon as the Indians were convinced that he was brave and honest, some red warrior in the village chose the trader as his particular friend and charge. With due ceremony, the two men exchanged names, and sometimes clothes, as a pledge of their friendship and loyalty. Many times a trader was saved from torture and death by the protection of his special friend.

The Indians called on the trader in their village for all kinds of services, even to doctoring them when they were ill. Doctoring, however, was not a safe trade to follow, for if the patient died his friends would blame the doctor and sometimes his very life was in danger. Once an old Natchez warrior, who was "blind in one eye and very dim-sighted in the other," insisted that Adair must treat his eyes, and even went so far as to set the day for the treatment. Adair protested that he knew nothing about eyes, but the old warrior would not take "No" for an answer. The day for the treatment came, and so did the warrior. Adair knew nothing better than to try a mixture of fine burnt alum and "roman vitriol" (copper sulphate). The warrior stretched himself out on the bed with all the ceremony proper for such an occasion and Adair, filling a quill with the powder, blew it into the patient's eye. Instantly the warrior bounded up and jumped about, saying very hard things about the white man's medicine. Adair does not tell what effect his treatment had upon the Indian's eye, but probably he treated the blind eye, and all that the Indian suffered was a smarting or burning sensation.

The trader's journeys between the Indian villages and the settlements were full of danger, not only from wild animals but from enemy Indians who were always wandering through the Valley.

Once Adair was traveling alone through the country of the Choctaws, who were not on friendly terms with the Chickasaws in whose towns he was living. While he was making his camp for the night, up came two young Choctaws, bent on mischief if they found one white man all alone, but afraid to tackle more than one. Adair guessed what was in their minds and told them that his traveling companion, who was an expert shot, had stopped to kill a deer.

Not knowing whether to believe this or not, the

Choctaws sat down to wait for the companion who was such a good shot. Minutes went by and the friend did not come. When they had waited a long time they remarked that the friend must be lost or killed. Adair assured them that he was often late, for he quite frequently stopped to barbecue the meat so that it would not spoil. The Indians, still doubtful, left, saying they would return.

They came back, bringing a third Indian with them. When they found that Adair's friend still had not come, they said "the ugly white man stayed long." Adair replied that he often did not come until late in the night, and finished spreading bear and buffalo skins for two beds. When the Choctaw warriors saw the two beds and Adair's calm manner, they believed that he really did expect someone at any minute, and they gave up all thought of attack that night and left saying they would return in the morning and asking Adair to call them when his friend arrived. This Adair readily promised to do, but the red men had no sooner left than Adair left too. When his callers returned to the camp in the morning, he was many miles away and too far for them to pursue him.

Even if the trader was a successful doctor and could escape the deep-laid plots of the red men, he was never free from danger. In fact, his work was perhaps the most dangerous of pioneer days, and unless he was unusually brave and clever he could hardly hope very long to escape death. At any moment on the trail his pack-train might be surrounded by enemy Indians, his horses stolen, packs plundered, and himself killed.

In his own home, danger lurked on every side; and he never slept without his gun by his side. If an Indian in his own village became angry, he would not hesitate to kill the white trader. The whole tribe with which he was living were quite willing to take revenge on him if his people, the English, provoked them in any way. Nor was he spared if an enemy tribe attacked the village in which he lived.

But as a rule, the Indians tried to protect their trader and he them. When white men began to live in the Indian country, the trader was often the "go-between" with the settlers and Indians and prevented many massacres. If he chanced to hear the Indian chiefs plotting an attack, he found some way to warn the white settlements. Even Indian friends themselves have been known to warn the trader so that he, in turn, might get word to his people of a proposed attack. If a white man was taken captive it was often the trader in the village who saved his life or gained him his freedom.

The discoverers and explorers won fame because they were the first to do the things they did. The tasks they did were often no harder and no more dangerous than those of the trader who for the first time followed the trading path, who fearlessly met the suspicious Indians and won their friendship, and who faced alone the dangers of the unbroken wilderness. The traders led the way for the settlers to follow into the Valley.

II
Trading Posts and Forts

WHEREVER EXPLORERS LINGERED in the land of the western waters, rude shelters were put up to protect them from storms and from the perils of the wilderness. When explorations gave place to the Indian trade the shelters at the meeting places were strengthened for trading posts and forts. The forts were very different in size and importance. Some were small huts like Fort Prudhomme, which La Salle hastily built to protect his party from the Chickasaws; some were large stone forts built for military purposes.

The French, on their way down the Great Valley, started trading centers along the Mississippi River and its tributaries. The Spanish built military posts along the coast of Florida to protect their settlements from the Indians and from their French and English enemies. The English forts were built mainly for the protection of the Indian trade, and extended along the trading paths from Charleston and Savannah and other Carolina and Virginia towns into the country of the Cherokee and Creek nations. The hunting grounds of the "civilized nations" of Indians became a network of trading paths protected by the forts of three rival European powers.

As the white men came nearer and nearer, the Indians, too, began to feel the need of forts in which to leave the old men, women, and children while the warriors were off on the warpath attacking their red and white enemies. The French and the English saw here a chance to win the allegiance of the Indians by building, or promising to built, forts in their country.

The Encircling French

The French had found in the fur trade of the Valley a true gold mine, and they naturally were jealous of the English traders over the mountains who were beginning to find their way into the Valley. La Salle, when he came down the Great River, had been quick to see that if the French were to hold the Valley, they must plant colonies there. His own attempt, however, to make a settlement at the mouth of the river had failed.

But the French still believed that they could keep out the English by building the chain of forts which

La Salle had planned. French fur traders selected the best locations for their trade centers, and the French government built the forts. Or, as sometimes happened, the Indians became so troublesome that forts had to be built for defense. Slowly, fort by fort, the circle grew. Fort Frontenac was built at the outlet of Lake Ontario in 1673, before La Salle started on his search for the mouth of the Mississippi River; Fort Niagara on the Niagara River, in 1678–79; and Fort Miami, on the southern end of Lake Michigan, in 1679, while La Salle was waiting for the arrival of his ship, the "Griffon." La Salle built Fort Crèvecoeur in 1680 on the Illinois River, where it widens into Peoria Lake, among the friendly Illinois Indians, and Fort St. Louis was built by Tonty in the same year on the famous Starved Rock of the Illinois River between Fort Miami and Fort Crèvecoeur. You will remember that Fort St. Louis was destroyed by the Iroquois Indians in their war against the Illinois and was rebuilt by La Salle and Tonty in 1682. There a large trade in buffalo skins was carried on among the Illinois Indians.

On his way down the Mississippi River, La Salle hastily built the little Fort Prudhomme on the Chickasaw Bluffs in 1682, and later, in 1685, when he brought his colony from France and missed the mouth of the Mississippi, he built another Fort St. Louis, on Matagorda Bay.

Then fort-building stopped in the lower Mississippi Valley until Iberville came to carry on La Salle's work, and built Fort Mobile in 1702 near the mouth of the Alabama River.

Whenever the French started a trading center, they stationed army officers there, and gave them control of the trade in the section which the fort commanded. At Fort Mobile the officers had their homes, a chapel in which to hold religious services, and a parade ground where the soldiers could drill. Upon the walls of the fort were mounted four guns, which made the French Indians feel safe and made their enemies afraid to attack.

A small fort was built by Iberville near the mouth of the Mississippi River shortly after he came to Louisiana, and was named New Orleans, but the settlement of New Orleans was not established until 1718 by Iberville's brother, Bienville.

You have read how the Natchez Indians and the Chickasaws troubled the French trading canoes on the Mississippi River. Iberville saw that another fort was needed there and selected the site of Fort Rosalie, which Bienville later built in 1716 where the city of Natchez now is. This was a "sorry little fort with only two guns," wrote an officer, but it served to quiet the Indians, and a thriving little village called Natchez grew up around it. The fort was rebuilt later and made larger and stronger.

As the rivalry with the English traders increased, the French built more forts nearer the Chickasaws and Cherokees. Fort Toulouse was one of these. It was built in 1717 at the junction of the Coosa and Tallapoosa rivers, to hold the friendship of the Upper Creeks. It was just a plain wooden fort, but it soon became a center of French activities in the Valley. The Indians took their furs there for trade, and the Jesuit missionaries went out from there to work among the neighboring Indians. Spies and messengers who were to be sent into the Cherokee country went to Fort Toulouse to get their orders.

Year by year the French trade with the Indians grew, and the Indians became accustomed to seeing French officers and *coureurs de bois* in their towns. Fort Tombigbee was established by Bienville in 1735 in the heart of the Choctaw country on the Tombigbee River, above the mouth of the Black Warrior River. It was a strong wooden fortress and was a help to the French in their fur trade and a protection to the Choctaws against their enemies, the Chickasaws.

One Indian nation, however, never became reconciled to having the French in their country—the

Chickasaws. When Bienville, the French officer at Mobile, decided that the Chickasaws must be destroyed if the interests of King Louis were to be saved, he erected two forts from which to conduct his military operations. Fort Assumption, built in 1739 on the Mississippi River where Memphis, Tennessee, now is, did not last long, for the French abandoned it when they made peace with the Chickasaws in the same year. But Fort Tombigbee was kept as a means of holding the friendship of the Choctaws.

In the next twenty years the French added no important new forts to their chain in the South. But northward, in the Ohio Valley, where the French and the English were having one war after another in their fight for the fur trade of the Great Lakes and the Ohio Valley, French fort-building went on briskly. In 1719 a cousin of Bienville, named Pierre Boisbriant, was sent up the Mississippi Valley from Mobile to build a fort among the Illinois Indians to keep the English away from the lead mines in that region. This fort was completed the next year and was named Fort Chartres. It was built one mile from the Mississippi River, but it is said that today the river flows over the place where the fort once stood. It was sixteen miles above the French mission of Kaskaskia and about the same distance from another French mission called Cahokia. On the Wabash River, where the English were also working their way in, a little French trading post was fortified by Sieur de Vincennes in about 1731 and named for him.

Both France and England wished to control the Ohio River, and in 1753 the French built Fort Le Boeuf on one of the streams flowing into the Allegheny River, the northern fork of the Ohio. A few months later they built Fort Machault (or Venango) forty miles south of Fort Le Boeuf, on the Allegheny River. Governor Dinwiddie, of Virginia, said that these forts were in Virginia territory, and, as you will read later, sent the young George Washington to protest against them.

But still the French pushed on. In the next year, 1754, they came down the Allegheny River in their canoes and captured a fort which the English had started to build at the Forks of the Ohio (where the Allegheny and Monongahela rivers come together to form the Ohio River, and where Pittsburgh now is). They made the fort larger and stronger and named it Fort Duquesne. This marked the beginning of the great French and Indian War, which ended by driving the French out of the Mississippi Valley. It was fought mainly in the North, but the Cherokees played an important part in it, as you will see.

During the French and Indian War, after the English had won back Fort Duquesne, the French made one last effort to hold the Ohio River, and in 1757 they built Fort Massac on the Ohio near the place where the Tennessee River flows into it. This was the last fort that the French built in their attempt to encircle the English. As it turned out, their brave chain of forts was not strong enough to hold the English behind the Blue Wall. By the end of the French and Indian War, in 1763, the English held all the forts in the Valley, including Kaskaskia and Vincennes (later named Fort Sackville), which George Rogers Clark captured during the American Revolution.

The English Forts

While the French were building their forts and trading posts in the Great Valley, the English were driving their pack-trains to and fro between the eastern settlements and the western Indians.

At first the English built their forts and trading posts at the fall lines of their coastal rivers, at the head of navigation. Fort Henry, from which Needham and Arthur started out, was one of these early forts. It was built in 1645 at the falls of the Appomattox. It was like the other forts of the time, which were built on the principal rivers to protect the settlers from the Indians and to be centers of the fur trade. Fort Charles on the James River, which was the beginning of Richmond, was especially well known. Fort Henry, you will remember from the story of Needham and Arthur, was on the great Occoneechee Trading Path, which led southwest into the country of the Catawba Indians and the Lower Cherokees.

As time went on, the South Carolinians needed forts more than the Virginians did. South of them were the Spaniards, fighting hard to hold Florida and to share in the fur trade of the Great Valley. West of them were the French, friends of the Choctaws and always working among the Creeks and the Cherokees to win them away from the English.

In South Carolina, the traders from Charleston usually followed a well-known trading path to the falls of the Savannah River, where from earliest days there had been an important Indian village and trading post. In 1716 Fort Moore was built here, not far from the present city of Augusta. At Fort Moore, the Charleston traders took the great inland trading path to the Cherokee and Creek nations. Here was an important junction of trading paths. The Occoneechee Path from the north joined the path to the Cherokee towns.

Two years later, in 1718, Fort Congaree was built on the Congaree River near the present city of Columbia. Here, too, the Occoneechee Path crossed a

Cherokee trading path, the one that led to the important Indian town of Keowee. When the path to Fort Moore became too dangerous because of Spanish and Indian attacks, the Congaree trail was more used by the fur traders.

Other small trading posts were scattered here and there east of the mountains, but the English built neither posts nor forts in the Valley beyond the Blue Wall until they saw that they would have to do it if they wished to hold the friendship of the powerful Cherokees and to protect their own advancing settlements against the raids of French Indians.

James Oglethorpe and the Indians

In 1733 another English colony was started in the South. James Oglethorpe brought a company of people to settle at Savannah, and this was the beginning of Georgia. Thus South Carolina had the help of Georgia in her fight against the Spaniards and the French Indians. Oglethorpe won the friendship of the Creeks who lived around Savannah. As Sir Alexander Cuming had done with the Cherokees, Oglethorpe took a party of Creeks to England, including his great friend, the Indian chief Tomo-chici. They, like the Cherokees, met the king and were entertained to their hearts' delight. When they went back to Georgia, they carried with them many presents and a high opinion of England's might and glory, which served the colonies well in the troubled times to come. Oglethorpe was a great help in dealing with the Indians.

From the very first, Georgia had to fight the battles of the English against the Spaniards and the French Indians. Spain owned Florida and claimed part of the land which had been granted to Georgia. Most of southern Georgia was therefore called the Debatable Land. Besides, the French, the Spanish, and the English all wanted the rich fur trade of the Creek Indians. The Spanish and the French sent agents among them to win them away from the English.

It was here that Oglethorpe showed his great skill in dealing with the Indians. He was able to hold their friendship for England. A half-breed Indian woman named Mary Musgrove helped him in this. She could speak English and she acted as his interpreter, helping to make treaties of trade and friendship with the Creeks. She also visited among the Creeks and brought parties of them to Savannah to greet Oglethorpe and to renew their vows of friendship.

On one of these visits, in 1739, the Indians told Oglethorpe that the French and the Spanish were working among them against the English, and they invited Oglethorpe to come to a great meeting of the

OGLETHORPE

Creeks, Cherokees, Choctaws, and Chickasaws at Coweta Town on the Chattahoochee. Oglethorpe went, although it was a hard and dangerous journey. With a small party of companions and with Indian guides, they traveled over two hundred miles along winding Indian trails, sleeping on the ground at night, with only a shelter of branches when it rained. When they came to rivers, they crossed by swimming or on rafts which they made from trees. But the journey was worth all the hardship, for Oglethorpe won the friendship of thousands of red men for England, at a time when they might have wiped out the English colonies if they had been unfriendly.

The War of Jenkins' Ear

Oglethorpe did more than win the friendship of the powerful Creeks; he finally drove the Spanish out of the Debatable Land. On his way home from Coweta Town, he stopped at Augusta, and here he learned that England had declared war on Spain.

In the southern colonies, this strange war was known as the War of Jenkins' Ear, because the Spaniards had caught a man named Jenkins smuggling English goods into Spanish ports and had cut off his ear, telling him to show it to the English King. Jenkins told all this to the King, and at the same time the English learned that the Spaniards were capturing and plundering English ships. This caused the declaration of war.

When Oglethorpe learned that England and Spain were at war, he did not wait for the Spaniards to attack the Georgia settlements. He sent runners into the Indian country to ask for a thousand warriors and he got together what few troops he could from South Carolina and Georgia. Then, with his red men, his Englishmen, and a troop of Highlanders, he boldly invaded the enemy's country. Part of his force marched overland to St. Augustine, and part went by sea, in nine small ships provided by the English navy. The plan was to attack St. Augustine by land and by sea at the same time, but the signals between the land and the sea forces did not work. The ships had trouble getting over the sand bars into the harbor, and the Spaniards had boats there to fight off invaders. Then Oglethorpe tried to starve out the Spaniards, but this, too, failed. Finally he was forced to give up and withdraw to Frederica on St. Simons Island. The great fort at St. Augustine was too strong for Oglethorpe's handful of colonial soldiers and red men.

Oglethorpe knew that it would not be long before the Spaniards attacked Georgia. So he worked hard to keep the English forts on the sea islands in repair and to hold the friendship of the Indians. He could get no help from England, and the South Carolinians were so disgusted with his failure to capture St. Augustine that they would do little to keep the Spaniards out of Georgia.

When the Spaniards finally started northward to attack Georgia, it was a little like the story of David and Goliath, with Oglethorpe as David. And, as in that story, the weaker side won the victory. The Spaniards' fleet started out from Havana and sailed to St. Augustine. Then they came northward destroying Oglethorpe's little forts, until they reached St. Simons Island.

Here the Spaniards landed and took possession of Fort St. Simon on the southern end of the island. But Oglethorpe and his men had retreated northward to the town of Frederica, and, when the Spaniards followed, they had to march in single file through a thick jungle with marsh grass on one side. Here they could easily be attacked, and there was a fierce battle of Spaniards, Highlanders, Indians, and Englishmen, which has ever since been known as the Battle of Bloody Marsh. Finally the Spaniards were defeated and withdrew. Although they were stronger than the English, they decided that they could not fight in the marshy jungle of St. Simons Island, and so Oglethorpe was victorious, and Georgia was saved for the English. It is said that "every governor from

New York through North Carolina congratulated and thanked Oglethorpe for delivering the mainland from the Spaniard." And now the English were free from the hindering presence of Spain in their westward drive for trade and power in the land of the western waters.

George Washington Climbs the Blue Wall

George Washington, like other great Virginians, was deeply interested in the lands beyond the mountains. He always preferred the life of woods and trails and camp-fires to the indoor life of towns. When he was just a boy, he learned surveying, and when he was only sixteen years old, he accompanied a surveying party sent out by Lord Fairfax beyond the Blue Wall. During the next few years, the young Washington traveled much in the wilderness with his chain and compass. He visited Indian villages and saw how the settlers lived. He always studied the country and noticed where the best lands were. In 1752, when he was only twenty years old, he was made an officer in the Virginia militia.

In the next year he was sent upon a most dangerous and unusual mission. The French, you will remember, had built Fort Le Boeuf and Fort Machault (or Venango), near the headwaters of the Allegheny River. This was in Virginia territory, and Governor Dinwiddie of Virginia resolved to send the French a warning. First he chose Captain William Trent, who started out, but, hearing that the French and Indians were advancing in large numbers, he turned back.

Then Governor Dinwiddie sent George Washington, age twenty-one, into a country full of Indians and hostile French. Washington started out with a small party and with Christopher Gist as guide. In heavy rain and snow they made their way through the wilderness. When they came to an Indian village, Washington held an important council-meeting with the Indian chief, Half-King. When he reached the French fort, he delivered Governor Dinwiddie's message.

The French officers treated Washington courteously, but they refused to withdraw. Washington, however, learned their plans and observed the forts, so that he was able to take back a good deal of useful information to Governor Dinwiddie.

The journey home was difficult and dangerous. Their horses gave out, and Washington carried a pack like the others. In this way they spent Christmas Day. The party traveled so slowly that Washington, who knew that he ought to get word to Governor Dinwiddie as soon as possible, decided to leave his party to come on as they could, and to go home "the

nearest way through the woods on foot." So, with his gun and his pack, he started out on December 26, accompanied by Christopher Gist. It was a thrilling journey. A French Indian tried to shoot Washington. When they were crossing the Allegheny River on a raft, amid floating chunks of ice, Washington was thrown into the icy water, and Gist had his hands frozen. They finally reached home safely, and Washington gave Governor Dinwiddie his account of the trip and told him what he had learned about the French plans.

In the next year the French and Indian War began in earnest, and Washington played an important part in it. He built a road across the mountains from Mills Creek (now Cumberland, Maryland), and in May he reached Great Meadows, beyond the Blue Wall, where he defeated a small body of French under Jumonville. Then, fearing an immediate French and Indian attack, he built Fort Necessity. This was the first fort beyond the Blue Wall to fly the English flag. Unfortunately it did not fly long, for Washington was defeated there a short time afterward.

Fort Cumberland was then built at Wills Creek, and it was now the westernmost fort of the English.

By this time the French had built Fort Duquesne at the Forks of the Ohio, and General Braddock was sent against it. Washington, now twenty-two, accompanied the expedition (as did also Daniel Boone, as hunter and waggoner). Braddock knew nothing about Indian warfare. He kept his soldiers massed in the open road, and the Indians and Frenchmen shot them down from behind trees. Braddock himself was so badly wounded that he died a few days later, and Washington took command. He managed the retreat so well, caring for the wounded and fighting off the Indians, that his fame as a soldier spread throughout the colonies.

When in 1758, General Forbes was sent against Fort Duquesne, Washington was with him, and helped to build Forbes's Road across the mountains, along which the English army marched. This time Fort Duquesne was taken, and was soon named Fort Pitt. Again the English flag flew above the Great Valley.

All his life Washington was greatly interested in the land beyond the Blue Wall, and when he became the first President of the United States, he realized the difficult problems of the pioneers and did his best to solve them for the good of the entire nation.

Forts for the Cherokees

The French and Indian War of 1754–1763 was fought mostly north of the Ohio River, but the southern end of it was the Cherokee War, which started in this way. The Cherokee nation was full of French spies and agents. South of the Cherokee towns, the French Indians were a constant threat of danger, and the Cherokees, who were allies of the English, became restless and fearful of attacks, especially upon their women and children when the Indian braves were on the warpath.

Old Hop, the Emperor, complained that the English did not give them enough ammunition and that his people could not fight with their fists, for the French wore shoes and would kick them, which would not be agreeable. Anxious to keep them friendly, Governor Glen of South Carolina held a meeting in 1753 and invited the Indians to tell all their troubles. The Cherokees proposed to give land for forts if the English would hurry up and build them. Then, they reasoned, their women and children and their old men would be protected while the warriors went on the warpath against their Indian and white enemies who seemed to surround them.

Governor Glen promised a fort in the Lower Cherokee towns on the Savannah River and, true to his word, in that same year, erected Fort Prince George. Though the Indians were pleased with this large wooden fort within a stone's throw of the Cherokee town of Keowee, they still wanted more.

When Virginia asked Old Hop for warriors to help fight the French in the French and Indian War, he refused unless the English would build them a fort. So Virginia and South Carolina agreed to build one together. But the Indians decided they wanted two forts instead of one. Then Old Hop promised to send four hundred warriors to help fight the French, and in return Virginia sent Major Lewis and sixty men to build the fort at once. With his men, Major Lewis arrived at Chota, the Cherokee capital, late in June, 1756. Old Hop and Little Carpenter—the Ouconecau who went to London, also known as Atta Kulla Kulla—went out to meet them, greeted them most cordially, and made them feel at home. Work on the fort moved rapidly, and in less than three months it was finished. Major Lewis, ready to go back to Virginia, asked for his four hundred warriors, but Old Hop seemed to have forgotten his promise. When he was reminded of it he merely made another—that he would send two hundred warriors when the governor of Virginia sent some soldiers to guard the fort. But the governor sent no soldiers and Old Hop sent no warriors, and a few months later the new fort was destroyed.

Meanwhile the Overhill Cherokees did not forget that the governor of South Carolina had promised them a fort. They grew impatient and Little Carpenter reproved Governor Glen sharply, saying that though he once had thought the governor a very great warrior he now seemed to him as no more than a little boy. At last, however, a site was selected near Little Carpenter's own town, where the Tellico River empties into the Little Tennessee, a splendid location at the gateway of the whole country.

In October, 1756, Captain Raymond Demeré, who was to be in charge of the work, arrived with two hundred men at Tomatley, and their coming was made a gala occasion by the Overhill Cherokees.

Fort-building in the Wilderness

Building a fort in the wilderness was a great undertaking under ordinary conditions, but building one during war times was doubly hard. The soldiers had to be protected from enemy Indians who might be passing through, and the friendly Indians had to be protected from thoughtless soldiers who were likely to think the whole country was theirs and rob the Indian fields when in search of food.

Under this constant guard and protection the work at the fort went on. It seemed very slow to the Indians, but this was to be no mere log structure but a stone fort surrounded by trenches, with mounted cannon at its corners. Nothing filled the Indians with more respect than the boom of cannon mounted on walls that would resist their bullets and their arrows.

The stone for the fort was blasted from the rock in the hillside, and deep trenches were made in the same way. With the blowing up of rock and the arrival of iron from over the mountains, the Indians began to fear that the English were planning to kill them or make them slaves. Some of the French Indians had told them that the iron was to make slave collars. When the English told them it was for the blacksmith shops for which the Indians had begged, and that the trenches were merely to protect the

fort, they were satisfied and watched the work closely day after day. Some days it seemed to go so slowly that they feared the French would come before it was finished. Old Hop said he feared nothing for himself for his life was not more than an inch long, but when he saw a white man his heart beat and his flesh trembled to think what might happen to him.

The twelve cannon upon the bastions pleased the Indians more than anything else, for they liked the loud noise of the big guns. To them a salute from the cannon meant more than presents. The guns were almost as much a matter of pride to the English soldiers as to the Cherokees, for they had been brought across the Blue Wall from South Carolina on the backs of horses, a distance of several hundred miles, much of it through a wild rugged mountainous region. Even at the slow pace of six miles a day, a gun would sometimes catch upon the trees, twist upon the saddle on which it was fastened, and cause the horse to plunge down to its death.

At one time the work on the fort came to a complete standstill. De Brahm, the engineer, ran away one night in December and left the fort unfinished. Old Hop ever after called him "the warrior who ran away in the night." However, the fort was completed in June, 1757. It was called Fort Loudoun, or Loudon, in honor of the Earl of Loudoun who had recently come to America.

The Indians were very proud of this fort, which overlooked their river and whose great guns boomed out their protection of the Overhill towns. Now they were ready to do anything for the Great Father, King George.

Traders and hunters began to come to the Little Tennessee River and build their homes in the shadow of the fort. There soon grew up a thriving little village and the Indians and white men lived together in peace.

English Blundering

But peace and security did not last long in the eastern valley for all Indians are sensitive and quick to take offense. The Cherokees were especially so, for they were a very proud nation. In the fall of 1758, during the French and Indian War, Little Carpenter with other warriors went to the Ohio country to help General Forbes drive the French from the Virginia frontier and from Fort Duquesne, at the Forks of the Ohio. Unfortunately General Forbes knew very little about how to treat Indians. Little Carpenter deeply resented the indifference, ridicule, and injustice which they met in the British camp. "Why," he said indignantly, "General Forbes did not even give us so much as a little paint." So Little Carpenter and his warriors simply turned around and went home, which to them was perfectly natural, for the Indians were accustomed to fighting only when they pleased. General Forbes, however, sent his soldiers to overtake them and take away their guns and hatchets.

Trudging homeward, out of sorts, they ran across some horses running loose and, according to their custom, took them. The settlers to whom the horses belonged started in pursuit of the Indians, and before it was over, blood of both whites and Indians had been spilled. The young warriors with Little Carpenter wanted to take the warpath immediately, but the older men persuaded them to wait and try to get satisfaction in some other way. They appealed to the governors of Virginia and South Carolina and were given presents, "to hide the bones of the dead and wipe away the tears from the eyes of their friends," as the red men expressed it. But the restless young men continued to worry the English frontiers, and when, on one of their raids, they killed two soldiers of the Fort Loudoun garrison, war seemed certain.

The governors of Virginia and South Carolina sent word to Little Carpenter that these young fellows would have to stop their scalping or their Father-over-the-Water would send his whole army to wipe out their villages. Little Carpenter, who still remembered his visit to King George, tried his best to prevent war. Oconostota, the Great Warrior, and Outacite, Judge's Friend (or Judd's Friend), with twenty-six other warriors, went to Charleston to see Governor Lyttelton, to try to make terms of peace. The governor refused to consider any terms until the Indians who had killed the soldiers were brought in for punishment. He promised the warriors a safe return to their towns, but the promise was not kept and the warriors were taken to Fort Prince George and put in prison, where they were held as hostages until the Indian murderers were brought in.

The Indians did not understand the meaning of the word "hostages"; to them it meant slavery. Even Little Carpenter could not understand or explain to his people why warriors who had done the English no harm and who were really seeking peace should be thrown into prison. Little Carpenter persuaded Governor Lyttelton to release Oconostota, their chief warrior, with five others. It was now too late, however, for war flamed up hotly.

The Cherokees refused all offers of peace and sounded the war cry in earnest. No amount of presents could satisfy them. The young warriors were out for blood, and this time they had the consent of the older men—all except Little Carpenter, who, rather than have any part in the raids on his English friends, retired with his family to the woods.

Oconostota, resentful of his unfair treatment, was determined to destroy Fort Prince George. One day, pretending he was on a peaceful errand, he persuaded Lieutenant Coytmore, the commander at the fort, to come to the river bank to talk to him. The lieutenant, suspecting nothing, went down to meet him. Just as he reached the edge of the river Oconostota gave the signal to his warriors in ambush and they shot him, wounding him so badly that he died shortly after. The war between the English and the Cherokees was on in earnest now.

The Siege of Fort Loudoun

The siege of Fort Prince George which followed the murder of Lieutenant Coytmore was unsuccessful. The Indians, still resentful, now turned their attention to Fort Loudoun and cut it off from all communication with the English.

In the little village around the fort, where red men and white had lived in peace and quiet, all was confusion. The trails were haunted by spies ready to shoot and scalp any messengers who might try to get to Fort Prince George. Scouting parties were sent to the north to prevent any communication between Virginia and the Fort Loudoun garrison.

Families of white settlers with household possessions gathered into the fort. Horses and cattle were driven into the enclosures, for no one knew how long the siege would last. The fort which had been intended for a protection to the Indian women and children was now a shelter for the English against the Indians for whom they had built it.

The Indians were unable to destroy the fort; so they decided to starve the English into surrender. Then they would have the fort and its guns. By using their provisions sparingly, the English had enough to last them twenty days. Had it not been for Indian women who were friendly to some of the soldiers, the English would have had to give in sooner than they did; but these loyal squaws secretly carried beans and corn into the fort until they were discovered. Lieutenant-Governor Bull of South

Carolina, knowing that the Indian women could not resist paint and ribbons, succeeded in getting two men through the Indian lines with those articles for the garrison to use for buying provisions. A yard of ribbon would buy corn enough to last one man a month.

For six months the siege continued, and no aid could be got through to the unhappy fort from either north or south. The soldiers and their families were reduced to eating their horses and dogs. Still hunger stared them in the face. The men were getting weaker and weaker. Some of them preferred leaving the fort and throwing themselves upon the mercy of the Indian tomahawks to dying by degrees as they were doing.

By August, 1760, their food supply was entirely exhausted, and Captain Demeré called a council of his soldiers. It was unanimously agreed to surrender, and Captain John Stuart, second in command, was chosen to go to Chota, the Cherokee capital, and make the best terms he could. He had always been a favorite with the Indians, who called him "Bushy Head"; so they listened quietly to all he had to say. It was agreed that the English should leave the fort on August 8 with their guns and enough ammunition to last them until they reached Virginia or Fort Prince George. They were to have as many horses as they needed and Indian escorts to see them safely into the English country.

On the day agreed upon, the inhabitants of the fort marched out and the Indians took possession. The English, traveling to Fort Prince George, camped after a journey of eighteen miles. Before morning their Indian guides left them and Captain Demeré sensed trouble. He called his men to arms, but, before they had a chance to line up, the Indians fell upon them, killing and scalping without mercy. Captain Stuart and some of the soldiers escaped the tomahawk, but were taken back to Fort Loudoun and made prisoners.

Little Carpenter, Friend of the English

As soon as Little Carpenter heard that Captain Stuart was a prisoner among his people, he returned from his exile in the woods; and, after much bickering with Stuart's captors, succeeded in buying him, paying for him all the treasures he had, clothes, knives, and rifle. Though Stuart was a captive, Little Carpenter treated him with great kindness and consideration.

Oconostota, the Great Warrior, was still bent upon attacking Fort Prince George. He unfolded to Stuart a plan for taking the cannon from Fort Loudoun to Fort Prince George and for having Stuart train and fire them against his own people. This plan Stuart confided to Little Carpenter, boldly saying that he would never consent to it. Little Carpenter, taking him by the hand said, "Captain Stuart, I have always been a friend to the English, I still am, and I shall always be."

The next day Little Carpenter told the Indians that he was going hunting and was taking his prisoner with him to feed him up on venison which he had not had since his capture. As soon as they got far enough from camp not to be discovered they headed toward Virginia. After marching nine days and nights they met Colonel Byrd on his way to help the garrison at Fort Loudoun, but it was too late and all returned to Fort Byrd on the Monongahela River.

Though the Cherokees had gained the surrender of Fort Loudoun and the possession of the great guns, which they admired but did not know how to use, they could not long hold out against the English. Through the efforts of Little Carpenter peace was made, and the Cherokees again became English subjects. Peace reigned once more in the land of the westward-flowing waters.

Part VI
OCCUPYING THE WILDERNESS

12

The Hunters in the Forest

UNTIL THE COMING of the white men the country between the Ohio and Tennessee rivers was held by the Indians as a game preserve and hunting ground. No Indians were allowed to live in it, but both northern and southern tribes hunted there at their pleasure. The Indians were very proud of this their national park and well they might be, for it abounded in wild game of all kinds—elk, deer, buffalo, bear, squirrels, and wild turkeys. In its dense thickets of cane-brake, laurel, and rhododendron, in its tangled masses of wild grape and pea-vines, lived also the more dangerous and less desirable animals—panther, wolf, and wildcat, as well as the rattlesnake and all kinds of creeping things.

Through the forests ran a network of trails, tracks, and traces—trails made by the ceaseless tracking of the buffalo and elk to and from the salt licks which were scattered through the forests; tracks of the smaller animals in their search for food and shelter; traces made by the Indians as they followed the buffalo trails in pursuit of game or of enemies.

The Shawnees, Creeks, and Cherokees who hunted in these forests had no desire to share their game with the white men. So when they found the white men's hunting camps or met the hunters on the trail, the Indians felt that they had a right to take from the strangers everything they had. One day some Shawnees, coming upon a party of hunters, took their pelts and said, "Go home and stay there. Don't come here any more, for this is the Indian hunting ground; and all the animals, skins, and furs are ours, and if you are so foolish as to venture again, you may be sure the wasps and yellow-jackets will sting you severely."

The white men went home but they did not stay there. Each year they braved the stings of the wasps and the yellow-jackets in greater and greater numbers until, by 1750, many groups of white men from the back settlements of Virginia and North Carolina were roaming the forest trails in the Indian hunting ground. The harvesting of pelts was to them an easier and more interesting way to earn a living than clearing land and planting crops. The independent adventurous life of the hunter was more to their liking than home life in the settlements.

The Life of the Hunter

As soon as the first cold winds of October came, these hunter-woodsmen began to get restless and look longingly toward the western forests. Everything at home seemed wrong—the houses were too hot, the feather-beds were too soft, or the children were too noisy, and the women could do nothing to suit them. Unable to endure the monotony of settlement life any longer, they answered the call of the woods, loaded their horses with provisions and camp equipment, and set out on the trail to the wilderness where neither white man nor Indian lived.

Dressed in a dark hunting shirt of deer-skin or linsey, which extended half-way to the knees, with long leather leggings, the hunter was protected against thorns, briars, and snake bites. With tomahawk thrust under his belt at the right, at the left a long sharp hunting knife, a powder horn, and bullet pouch, and with a long rifle slung across his shoulder, he was ready for the first deer, bear, or buffalo that crossed his trail.

Into the wide bosom of his hunting shirt he stuffed a chunk of bread and jerked meat, some tow for the rifle, and any other small trifles which he might need before he pitched his camp. In his shot-pouch were packed an awl and a roll of buckskin or "whanga"—

sinews of deer for making or mending moccasins after the day's hunt. Sometimes the hunter decorated his hunting shirt with tassels of shredded deer or elk skins and when he wanted a string for anything he just pulled it from the tassel. As he strode through the forests he made scarcely a sound, so lightly did he tread in his soft deer-skin moccasins, which in winter were stuffed with loose deer hair, wool, or leaves to protect the feet from the cold.

From early fall until late spring the hunters, going in groups of at least two, and often more, followed the trails of the fur bearers. Some of them believed that the furs were better in the months whose names had the letter "r" in them; and, certainly, the danger of Indian attacks was less during the "r" months.

When they reached the region where they chose to hunt, the hunters chose a secluded nook in a little valley to build the station camp, as they called it. Here they would be protected from the cold winds and at the same time would be less easily discovered by the Indians. Hardly a day was necessary to prepare the camp, for it was only a three-sided cabin or "lean-to" built against the trunk of a large tree which they chopped down for the purpose. When the sides and roof were covered with bark or animal skins, much of the cold wind was shut out and it was quite comfortable. Anyway, it provided them with a place

to sleep, to store their food, and to keep the pelts until they had enough to load onto their horses and take back to the settlements.

Evenings in the camp were enjoyable, too. Over the log fire in front of the open side of the cabin they cooked a hearty meal of buffalo meat or venison, or perhaps of 'possum, wild turkey, or some other forest delicacy, to which they added, as long as it lasted, a bit of the food they had brought from their settlement homes. The meal over, they sat around the fire and told stories while they mended their moccasins or cleaned their guns, the log fire lighting their rude shack. If some one of them had been able to squeeze a book into his closely packed baggage, one of the group read aloud while the others worked.

One evening when Daniel Boone and four others were camped on a small river in Kentucky not far from a Shawnee Indian village one of them read aloud the story of Gulliver's adventures in Lorbrulgrud in the land of the Brobdingnags. A day or so later Alexander Neely, who had listened to the story, returned to camp dangling two Shawnee Indian scalps and explained, "I have been to Lulbegrud and killed two Brobdingnags in their capital." To this day the little stream that ran through this Shawnee village where Neely killed the savages is called Lulbegrud Creek.

But the nights were not always spent in reading and story telling. The skins which the hunters gathered had to be prepared for the market. Each skin was scraped and rubbed until it was soft and pliable and could be easily packed. As they were finished, the skins were laid in piles across the poles raised several feet above the ground. Pelt by pelt and layer by layer, the piles grew until there were enough skins to be rolled into a bale. When all the skins had been made ready, the bales were bound in elk-skins and loaded onto the horses, and the hunters started on the homeward trail. One horse-load of a hundred pelts was worth about one hundred dollars and would buy many pounds of salt and other provisions for the hunter's family—if he got back to the settlement before the Indians found him.

The wild beasts in the western forests were so regular in their habits that the hunters soon learned when, where, and how to find them. In clear weather the deer, whose skins were so valuable, could be found on the highest ground in the open country, but in stormy weather the hunters sought them on the leeward side of the hills where they went for protection. The best time to hunt them, however, was at moonrise or in the early morning when they went to the salt licks and to their feeding places, for they were much easier to see in the thickets when they were on the move.

In winter the elk were found in their "mossing places" or "gardens" where they fed upon lichen, moss, and buds of shrubs and young trees. But the buffalo traveled from place to place and in large herds. The noise they made was like the roll of thunder and the earth shook under their tread. Woe unto the man, white or red, who got in the way of the buffalo herd. A hunter was once caught in this way and crushed under the feet of the buffalo. For five days his body lay hidden from his searching friends, so dense was the thicket where he had fallen.

In the fall after the buffalo had fed upon wild peavines and clover and the bear had fattened upon nuts and wild fruit, their meat was delicious and they were killed for that only, for their skins were too bulky to pack so great a distance. The elk meat was considered as good as venison, but the skins were used only for packing the bales of deer-skins.

After the white men east of the mountains found the Indian hunting ground, they came in increasing numbers each year until soon the buffalo herds grew smaller and the deer and other game more and more scarce. The plains and hills that once had been their feeding places became the white man's fields, and their paths and trails the white man's highway.

Long Hunters

In the English settlements there were some men who were able to spend more than one hunting season in the forests. Sometimes they stayed in the wilderness for a year or two, and because they hunted so long without returning home they were called Long Hunters. The first men to be called Long Hunters were James Knox and his party, who came into the land of the western waters in 1769 or 1770, but since then the name has been applied to all who went into the forests to hunt for a long time.

The Long Hunters were expert woodsmen and excellent judges of land values. For this reason they were often employed by prospectors back in the east-

ern settlements to report on land that would be good for clearing. Before the Cherokee War of 1758 and twenty years before James Knox and his party got the name of Long Hunters, a hunting party came into the Indians' national park with Dr. Thomas Walker, a surveyor and explorer from Virginia.

Coming down the Holston River through the Cherokee country and up through the Cumberland Gap, they hunted and explored for five months, camping along the Holston River and on Reedy Creek, which empties into the Holston at the foot of Long Island, now Kingsport, Tennessee. The country was covered with cane-brakes, and, as they rode along, the horses snatched mouthfuls of the cane and liked it.

From the time Dr. Walker led his party over the mountains in 1750 until fifteen or twenty years later when the stream of settlers began to come, many parties of hunters and explorers came into the Indian game preserve. Some were looking for land upon which to settle; others came for the profit to be made from hunting; while still others came for the sport of adventuring into the unknown new country. They often made their own trails, and where they found land which they specially liked, they laid claim to it by notching the trees with their hatchets.

In 1766 James Smith, who as a youth had been

captured by French Indians and had spent several years among them, came into the wilderness with Joshua Horton, who had with him his eighteen-year-old Negro slave named Jamie, and others. After exploring the country along the Cumberland and Tennessee rivers, Smith decided he would return to his home. At the mouth of the Tennessee River the party separated. Smith gave his horse to Joshua Horton and his friends, who were going on into the Illinois country. Horton, in turn, not wishing to see Smith go over the mountains alone, lent him the Negro boy to accompany him as far as Horton's home in Virginia.

Soon after he had left the group, Smith ran a splinter of cane into his foot. After several days it became so swollen and so painful he could walk no farther, and he decided that something must be done. The only instruments with which Smith could remove the splinter were a moccasin awl, a hunting knife, and a bullet mould. He made up his mind he would have to do his best with them.

With all the courage he had, Smith stuck the awl into the flesh, cut around the piece of cane with his hunting knife, and had the Negro pull out the cane with the bullet mould. Taking the jelly which the boy had made by boiling the root of a "lynn" tree, he bound it to his foot with moss and bark. To protect them from the weather, while his foot was healing, he directed the Negro boy to put up a rude shelter. They were alone in the wilderness, except for the Indians, whom they wished to avoid.

After some weeks Smith was able to walk again, and they made their way back to the settlements. When Smith reached home after an absence of eleven months he was so thin and his clothing so faded and torn that his family and neighbors did not recognize him. He could hardly make them believe he had made the journey over the mountains on foot.

The following year Kasper Mansker, woodsman and Indian fighter, brought a large party of adventurers into the Valley. Among them were John Rains, Anthony Bledsoe, Bacon, and Drake. They hunted and explored, discovered licks, creeks, and mountains which they named for members of the party —Bledsoe's Lick, Mansker's Lick, and Drake's Pond. After eight or nine months the party broke up. Some went farther into the wilderness, and some returned to their homes. Mansker and two others, thinking they might find a better sale for their deer-skins in the South, loaded two canoes and two large boats and went down the Mississippi River to Natchez.

Many interesting tales can be told of these men who first braved the perils of the wilderness. There was the hunter, Russell, who was so nearsighted that he could not see the muzzle of his gun without a

white rag tied to the end of it, but he could shoot as straight and kill as many deer as anyone. Matthew Harmon, also a Long Hunter, was such a dead shot that the Indians believed he was in league with the devil because he killed so many of them and had so many escapes himself.

The stories of the heroism and daring of the few Long Hunters whose names we know are also the stories of the many whom we do not know, but whose courage and daring contributed much to the opening of the land of the westward-flowing waters.

SINGING IN THE CANE-BRAKE

One evening as Kasper Mansker and other Long Hunters in the forest were sitting by their camp-fire, they heard a noise not far off which was not like anything they had ever heard in the wilderness—neither Indian nor buffalo nor wild turkey could make that sound. Fearing it might be an Indian, they crept cautiously in the direction from which the sound came and peeped through the cane-brakes. There, flat on his back, lay Daniel Boone, singing lustily.

Boone, the prince of pioneers, was a born hunter, scout, and woodsman. Enthralled with the tales he heard of the country which the Indians called Kentuckee, he made up his mind that some day he would go to that place and see things for himself. He was so busy at home clearing land, planting crops, and going on expeditions against the Indians who were attacking the forts that it was 1767 before he made his first attempt to find the trail through the mountains, about which his friend, John Findley (or Finley), a Pennsylvania trader, had told him. He lost his way and returned home disappointed at not having found the hunter's paradise.

When he reached home, he found Findley, whom he had not seen for twelve years, waiting to show him the way through the Cumberland Gap. Boone, with his brother-in-law, John Stuart, and three others, with Findley as leader, followed the trail through the gap in the mountains. Daniel's brother, Squire Boone,

was to follow as soon as he had harvested his and Daniel's crops, bringing fresh horses and a supply of ammunition. After weeks on the trail the hunters viewed for the first time the wonderful land of Kentucky, which came to be called "the dark and bloody ground."

For weeks they hunted in peace and without seeing a single red man, but just as they were beginning to feel secure they were attacked and robbed of everything they had—all the skins they had gathered, their provisions, and even their horses. Findley and others of the party got discouraged and went home, but Boone and Stuart were not satisfied to return until they had made an effort to get back some of their property. Trailing the Indians and watching their chance, they succeeded in catching two of the horses, but before they could get out of reach the Indians had captured them.

Meanwhile, on the trail to the settlements Findley and his companions met Squire Boone with horses and powder and shot on his way to the hunters. Findley told Squire of their misfortune and had about persuaded him to turn back when Boone and Stuart, having escaped from their captors, came stumbling into camp. Squire, Daniel, and Stuart now decided to stay in the forest and continue their hunt. Then one day Stuart failed to return to camp and was never seen again, and Daniel and his brother Squire were alone in the wilderness. Later, when they had enough skins to make a horse-load, Squire took the skins to the settlement to sell them and with the money pay off all debts and return to the camp with more powder, shot, and provisions. While he waited for Squire's return, Daniel looked after the camp, cleaned the guns, and scouted around the forest, killing only what he needed for food lest his ammunition give out before the new supply came. It was at this time that Mansker heard him singing in the cane-brake.

After Squire joined him again, the Boones hunted for several months more, gathered another load of skins, and then started home, for Daniel had now been absent almost two years. On their way, however, they were attacked by a band of northern Indians who took from them not only all their pelts but their ammunition as well, so that when they got home they were poorer than when they started out. But at least no one could take from them their knowledge of the country they had seen, and Daniel Boone had already made up his mind to move his family to this land of plenty.

The Giant Hunter

In 1776, a year after the beginning of the American Revolution, Thomas Sharp Spencer left his home in the Kentucky settlements to go farther down the Valley. With him were his friend Holliday and others. When they found that the land on the Cumberland River was all that it had been reported to be, and more, they built cabins about half a mile west of Bledsoe Lick and planted corn. After some weeks all except Spencer and Holliday got tired and went back home. Finally, Holliday, too, became discontented and returned to his friends in the settlements. When he had packed his few things, he found he had lost his hunting knife. It was impossible to travel two hundred miles through the wilderness without a knife of some sort with which to skin and cut his meat; so Spencer, with true wilderness generosity, broke his knife in two and gave Holliday a piece of the blade.

Spencer was a perfect giant in size and in strength. At the same time he was most generous, gentle, and friendly, but quiet and reserved. When his friend Holliday left him he made his camp in the hollow of a large sycamore tree and lived there alone. For several months he neither spoke to nor saw a human being. His big feet have been the subject of many jokes. One is told of a hunter who was with De Mombreun, a Frenchman, hunting near the French Lick. De Mombreun went to Vincennes, in the Illinois country, and left the hunter to follow later. While working around his camp one morning, the hunter saw huge footprints and decided there must be a giant in the forest. The next morning he was awakened early by a terrific noise and the sound of running. He leaped out of bed, ran to the river, and swam across without even looking to see what the noise was, so sure was he that it was the giant whose footprints he had seen the day before. So it was, but the giant was only Spencer, and the noise was made by a buffalo dashing through the cane-brake with Spencer after him.

Spencer stayed in the West after the settlers came out and was a great help to them because of his great strength and fearlessness. As he was helping two men put up a cabin one day, he got sick and had to lie down before the fire, but he kept his eye on the work. As he saw the men struggling with a beam which they were trying to put in place on the roof he said, "If I weren't sick I could do it myself." This angered one of the men who was a great bully and always picking a fight, and he said, "I am a better man than you, any day." Spencer got up without a word, picked up the beam, put it where it belonged, and returned to his blanket. The bully said no more nor did he try again to pick a fight with Spencer.

At a community gathering one day two men got into a fight, and Spencer, who was of a peaceful disposition, stepped between them to separate them. Bob

Shaw, a bystander who was enjoying the fight, got mad and hit Spencer in the face. Spencer quickly picked him up by the nape of the neck and the waistband of his trousers, carried him to a high fence near by, and tossed him over into the field. It is said that when the poor fellow got his breath back, he said meekly, "Mr. Spencer, if you'll pitch my horse over, I'll be going."

Fond of the forests, ill at ease in houses and with people, Spencer continued to wander in the wilderness even after the settlers came to be his neighbors. He preferred the open skies to the roof of a house, and he enjoyed the companionship of wild things more than that of people, though he was always ready to help whenever he could.

13

Pushing Westward

BY THE PROCLAMATION of 1763 King George III of England forbade his subjects in the American colonies to settle west of the Allegheny Mountains, and again the Indians had their valley as their own. They did not keep it long, however, for, five years later at Fort Stanwix, they too signed a treaty and gave the region which is now Kentucky and part of Tennessee to King George.

No sooner had the news of the Treaty of Fort Stanwix reached the settlements than the home-seekers started over the mountains. Long Hunters returned with their families to occupy the "tomahawk rights" they had taken while on hunting trips; frontiersmen who, while fighting the Indians in the Cherokee War, had been impressed by the beauty of the country and by its fertile soil and abundance of game, went into the valley to spy out new sections of rich land; others were lured into the West by the tales of adventurers and hunters.

Following the clear swift-flowing streams, little bands of pioneers came down the winding valley of the Holston River. Through the valley watered by the quiet, peaceful Watauga, other families came in search of homes. In the winter of 1768 a hunting party on its way into the wilderness, passing through the North Holston Valley, saw no signs of a white man's habitation, but when they returned six weeks later there was a cabin in every clearing.

Captain Bean in Watauga

Early in 1769 Captain William Bean, who had hunted in the western forests with Daniel Boone, left his home in Virginia to go into the land of plenty. With their scant household goods, parched corn and salt, and a few farm implements, the Beans started their journey westward. Armed with rifle and hunting knife, Captain Bean led the pack-horse upon which Mrs. Bean rode. Often he had to clear the trail as he went. With them came the cow and the dogs.

Many days they traveled, alert to the slightest sound or movement in the thickets. Following the hunting trail along the Watauga River, they came to Boone's Creek and stopped. Bean doubtless said to himself, "We will build our cabin here. I have been

here before and know the land is good and game plentiful," for it was the exact spot upon which he and Boone had camped on their hunting trip.

Tethering the horse and the cow so that they would not wander off, Captain Bean began at once to clear a patch of land large enough for a rough shelter of boughs and bark. Then began the real work. He felled trees to furnish logs for the cabin, and at the same time, with ax and firebrand, he cleared space for a patch of corn. With mattock and maul he split the logs and, placing them end across end, he had soon completed a little cabin with doors of split oak on wooden hinges. At the first signs of cold weather the huge cracks between the logs were filled with mud clay mixed with grass or deer's hair. Into the rough cabin they moved with proud hearts. If they were lonely it was not for long, because over in North Carolina the people were getting restless under a government which they thought was unfair and were looking toward the unsettled West as a place of freedom and opportunity.

James Robertson Goes Prospecting

One of the many who were discontented in North Carolina was James Robertson, a young man with a keen appreciation of the land about him and a love for his countrymen. He had heard of the beautiful valley of the Watauga from his friend Daniel Boone and decided he would go prospecting there.

One morning early in 1770, armed with rifle, bullet pouch, powder horn, and hunting knife, Robertson mounted his horse and started over the mountains, taking with him only a sack of parched corn, a package of salt, blanket, hatchet, and tin cup. As he rode from the little Carolina village his friends called to him, "Be sure to find good springs and rich lands and enough to accommodate us all."

Through the unbroken forests he rode alone with only his horse and his thoughts for company. When evening came he stopped, made a simple camp, kindled a fire with his flint, and cooked his evening meal. Refreshed with food, he rolled himself in his blanket and lay by his camp-fire to rest after his hard day of travel. Night after night he lay out under the trees and stars, sometimes sleeping and sometimes just listening to the strange sounds of the wilderness.

At the summit of Stone Mountain, the climbing of which was a day's journey, he looked down into the Watauga Valley covered with forests through which ran little rivers like silver threads. To him it seemed to be the Promised Land.

In the distance he saw a column of smoke rising from the trees. Could it be a white man's cabin, or was it an Indian camp? Fearing the latter, he went cautiously down the mountain side and found to his great joy that it was a cabin—that of Honeycut, William Bean's first neighbor. As the guest of Honeycut, Robertson stayed in the West until he had marked off a site for his home, planted a patch of corn, and selected locations for his friends. When he was ready to return, Honeycut gave him enough food to last him until he could reach his home in North Carolina and bade him farewell.

Robertson had not gone far when the skies clouded over and since he could not see the sun and stars which were his compasses, he lost his way. The rain came and continued day after day so that he could not keep his gun and powder dry even under his blanket. His food supply gave out and, having no means of shooting game, he had to live upon roots and berries, which were very scarce.

Coming to a cliff over which he could neither lead nor ride his horse he turned it loose to find its own way while he himself stumbled on as well as he could. He had been wandering two weeks when two hunters found him rain-drenched and weak from lack of food. They took him to their camp, fed him, and as soon as he was able to go on gave him a horse and put him on the right trail.

When his friends learned of his return, they asked him many eager questions about the new country. Robertson gave them a full account of his adventures, omitting none of the hardships of traveling over a rough and uncertain trail. Undaunted by his stories of danger, sixteen families decided to return with him to the West. So the following year Robertson with his own family led the little band over the mountains.

This group of home-seekers braved the perils of the wilderness, the toil and hardships of mountain climbing, led by Robertson and his stalwart allies. The men, with rifles and hunting knives ready for use at the first signs of danger, led the pack-horses upon which were mounted the women and small children with the household goods. The older children drove the lean cattle and enjoyed the strange

sights, being careful not to loiter by the way or wander from the path.

As night came on, they selected a camping place where they could rest and have a real meal, for at noon they ate only enough to refresh themselves for the remainder of the day's journey, so anxious were they to get as far as possible while they had the sun to guide them.

When, after many days of hard travel, they reached Watauga, there was much rejoicing, and the settlers who were already there threw open their cabins to the new-comers until more cabins could be built. The next day all set to work to build homes for the seventeen new families. For days the forests echoed with the sound of axes, the crashing of trees, and the dull thud of mattock and maul as the men split the felled trees into logs the right size. Soon seventeen pioneer homes, rough but comfortable, were finished.

While James Robertson was leading his seventeen families into the Watauga country, John Carter and his companions went into the valley lying between the Holston and Clinch rivers—a valley which offered the home-seekers all they needed—streams, springs, and fertile soil. Cabins were put up, a little store was built from which Carter and his friend Parker kept the settlers supplied with the necessities for their households; and Carter's Valley, for so the new settlement was named, became a thriving village.

South and west of Watauga there was yet another valley well adapted to the settler's needs, the valley through which runs the Nolichucky River. The year after James Robertson and John Carter came over the mountains, Jacob Brown, a merchant from South Carolina, rode into the Nolichucky Valley. Upon his pack-horse he had a load of goods, which he exchanged for a lease on a plot of land, and here he built homes for himself and two other families.

Each year saw new families arrive in the Watauga Valley, Carter's Valley, and Nolichucky settlements. New cabins were built in these stockaded hamlets or "stations," and trails led through the forests from one to the other. These brave pioneers who ventured across the mountains became like one large family, and later all were known as the Wataugans.

Boundaries, Treaties, and Laws

In the early days of exploration and settlement no boundaries between states or sections of the country were clearly defined. When the backwoodsmen of Virginia and North Carolina went to Watauga they thought they were settling on Virginia soil and were under the protection of her laws. But in 1771, the settlers in the Watauga and Nolichucky valleys found that they were really in North Carolina territory, and the Carter's Valley pioneers discovered that they were in the hunting ground of the Indians.

The Wataugans were defenseless. Virginia disowned them, and North Carolina was at this time too busy with other things to pay much attention to them. The Indians, too, were angry at the loss of their land.

An Indian chief told Alexander Cameron, the superintendent of Indian affairs, that white people were coming into their hunting grounds in large numbers, their guns were rattling everywhere, and there were horse paths on the river both up and down. Whereupon the superintendent of Indian affairs told the Wataugans that they would have to move, and he offered them land in West Florida. But the backwoodsmen were not so easily dislodged, for they had built their cabins, cleared the land, and planted crops. Fortunately the most influential Cherokees liked the Wataugans and agreed that they should stay if they would promise not to move any farther into the Indian country.

Now that they belonged to no colony, the only thing the pioneers could do was to set up their own government, for they must have laws to protect themselves against horse thieves and lawless adventurers who were continually coming into or passing through their settlements. Robertson, always the leader, called a meeting of the men, and together they worked out a plan by which they could manage their own affairs without assistance or interference from former rulers east of the mountains.

Calling themselves the Watauga Association they appointed a committee of five of the most respected citizens in the villages. These five were to decide on all matters of importance, including cases of lawlessness and treaties with the Indians.

Though the Cherokees had consented to their staying on the land which they had cleared, the backwoodsmen wanted something more definite than Indian promises. So the first thing the Watauga Association did was to have a meeting with the Cherokees and lease their land for ten years, paying six thousand dollars in trade goods. The treaty was signed, and a day was set for the Indians to come to Watauga to get their blankets and cloth and to celebrate the friendship pact between them and the white men.

The day came and so did the guests—Indians, backwoodsmen, and white visitors from the settlements in the North. It was a gala occasion and all entered with hearty enthusiasm into the horse races, ball play, and other outdoor sports. Some of the visitors showed too much enthusiasm, for they got into a quarrel with the Indians, and somehow a Cherokee warrior was killed. The Cherokees immediately picked up their

JAMES ROBERTSON.

blankets and guns and went home angry. The Wataugans knew their silence meant trouble, for Indians had been known to go on the warpath for a less offense than this.

A council of the leading men was called, and it was agreed that Robertson should go alone to the Cherokee town of Chota and try to make peace with the angry chiefs. There was no time to be lost, for doubtless the warriors already were raising a war party. So Robertson mounted his best horse and rode down the valleys as speedily as caution would allow, never knowing at what minute he might be attacked. He reached Chota unharmed, and the Cherokee chiefs were so amazed to see him come alone and unafraid into their presence that they listened quietly to all he had to say.

Explaining to the red men that the murderers of their warriors were not Wataugans but were some lawless men from Wolf Hills in Virginia, Robertson promised that the Wataugans would find them if possible and punish them. The Indians, impressed by his courage in coming through the forest alone and honored at having the leader of the white men come to them, promised to forget the murder and to keep their warriors at home.

The Cherokees kept their promise, and for three years the Wataugans lived in peace. At a meeting with the southern Indians at Sycamore Shoals in 1775, the Wataugans purchased outright the land on which they had settled, so that there were no more boundary disputes. The Cherokees gave up forever another portion of their territory and retired into the hills.

Nolichucky Jack, Indian Fighter

When the Watauga settlement was in its second year, there rode into the quiet peaceful village, a tall,

JOHN SEVIER

slender young man who was later to become its chief defender against the red foe. John Sevier had come down the Shenandoah Valley on a hunting trip, and hearing of this settlement to the south decided to visit it. So impressed was he with the beauty and resources of the country that he made up his mind then and there to move his family down. Returning to his home in Virginia, he settled his business affairs as quickly as possible and moved southward.

Christmas Day in 1773 saw the population of Watauga increased by the entire Sevier family—John, his wife and two sons, his father, mother, brothers and sisters. At his home in Virginia Sevier had been a merchant, and when he came to Watauga he brought his merchandise on his pack-horses and opened up a store where he exchanged blankets, trinkets, and cloth for the skins which the Indians brought in. He also sold household necessities to the settlers.

Sevier had inherited from his French Huguenot ancestors the qualities that make for leadership—courage, steadfastness, and personal charm. He had not been in the settlement long before he was an acknowledged leader second to none but James Robertson. He had been farmer, innkeeper, and merchant. Now he was to add to his accomplishments one other —that of Indian fighter.

The year after he came to the Watauga Valley a war with the Indians known as Lord Dunmore's War broke out and Sevier, chosen by Lord Dunmore, governor of Virginia, to get together an army to protect the settlements, began his career as Indian fighter. From the battle of Kanawha in 1774, said to be the most hotly contested battle in Indian warfare, until the end of Indian hostilities in 1796, Sevier's life was one of almost constant contest with Indians. He raided towns and villages, made peace treaties with the old warriors, only to have them broken by the reckless young braves and lawless white settlers.

With two hundred of the best riflemen he could find, Sevier worked quickly, surely, and with a vengeance, not waiting for the Indians to attack the stockaded forts but surprising them in their own villages or on the warpath. Wherever he found enemy Indians he burned and destroyed without mercy, but to those who befriended the white men he was kind and generous.

At the cry of "Indians!" Sevier's band of riflemen would mount their horses, seize a blanket and wallet of parched corn, and gallop away. With as much speed as rough trails, deep ravines, and mountain passes would allow, they swooped down upon the Indian towns with a blood-curdling whoop, which was their signal of attack. Before the Indians had time to see what was happening, Sevier had finished his work of destruction and started back to the settlements.

In his swift action lay his success—thirty-five battles and thirty-five victories. The Indians, who gave him the name of Nolichucky Jack, came to dread him so that if they heard him coming they deserted their towns without returning the fight, but they admired and respected him, and when they wanted

some service rendered or dispute settled they would say, "Send us Sevier. He is a good man and will do us right." For more than twenty years he fought off the red men and prevented the destruction of the frontier homes by these jealous savages.

But not all of Sevier's days in the new country were spent in contests with the red men, for his new home in the bend of the Nolichucky River was the scene of much merrymaking. The large roomy log house was seldom without a guest, and on his beautiful plantation were held many horse races and barbecues. No stranger came into the settlement who was not welcomed in the Sevier house. Hardly was a frontier wedding complete without a feast in his hospitable home.

When James Robertson left Watauga to start a new colony on the Cumberland River, Sevier became the leader of the Wataugans. He represented them in public affairs, and was one of the most prominent men in the early history of the land of the western waters.

These Wataugans were a spirited people. They knew what they wanted and they were willing to endure great hardships to get it. But they believed that they had rights, too, and they thought that the government ought to help protect them from the Indians and aid them in other ways. After the Revolution, they felt that North Carolina, of which Watauga was a part, was neglecting them, and so they formed a state of their own. They named it the State of Franklin, in honor of Benjamin Franklin. Nolichucky Jack was president of this state for four years and worked hard for its welfare.

But the State of Franklin did not last. The United States government refused to recognize it as a state, and it had a troubled career. North Carolina, too, really wished to hold the allegiance of the people beyond the mountains, and so promised to take better care of them. Finally the Franklinites gave up their idea of a separate state and again became a part of North Carolina. When the territory of Tennessee was formed, the old State of Franklin was a part of it. And when Tennessee became a state, Nolichucky Jack was its first governor.

14
Farther Westward

IT WAS MORE than a century after Gabriel Arthur had been captured by the Shawnees in the Indian hunting ground that the white men began to make their homes in the Shawnee country. Settlers had gone over the Alleghenies to the valleys of the Holston, Watauga, and Nolichucky rivers, but none had gone beyond the Cumberland Mountains. Several attempts had been made, but the Indians had driven the settlers back each time, until in 1774 James Harrod and his companions succeeded in evading the Indians long enough to build a cluster of cabins beyond the Kentucky River.

In less than six months a messenger rode into the little village, which they had named Harrodsburg, and warned the settlers that the Shawnees with the northern Indians as aids were attacking the frontiers of Virginia and advised them to return to the protection of the forts at the settlements. James Harrod and his friends abandoned their town with the determination to return as soon as the Indians had been quieted. Indian attacks on the frontier were many, but none got so far as the deserted village over the Cumberland Mountains. When Harrod and the others returned the next year the cabins were still there and the little hamlet was never deserted again.

THE FOUNDING OF BOONESBOROUGH

About the same time that Harrodsburg was reoccupied by its hardy pioneers, Richard Henderson, a progressive and shrewd land prospector of North Carolina, with some business associates purchased from the southern Indians a large tract of land on the Ohio, Kentucky, and Cumberland rivers. At a conference with the Indians at Sycamore Shoals on the Watauga River, Henderson paid the Indians ten thousand dollars in trade goods for the land, which he in turn expected to sell to adventurous colonists east of the mountains.

No sooner had Henderson made the purchase than he began to look for someone who was a good woodsman and who could lead others into the undeveloped region. Who could be better than the fearless Daniel Boone? Henderson persuaded him to undertake the enterprise, and with twenty-nine other brave frontiersmen Boone began to cut the trail from the Holston country to the Kentucky River.

With axes they blazed the trail, cutting a path through the undergrowth. Indians attacked and killed some of them, but Boone and the others who escaped Indian bullets and tomahawks worked steadily on until the Wilderness Trail was ready for the steady stream of pioneers who were waiting to come into the West.

Fortifications were necessary to ward off the attacks of the angry Indians, for this was the common land of both northern and southern tribes. Though all hands were needed to build the fort and cabins, Boone sent a messenger to Henderson to warn him that if he wished to hold this land against the Indians he would have to come at once with men to occupy it. Henderson had purchased the land in good faith from the southern Indians, but there were red men in the North who claimed that the southern Indians had no right to sell it and they were not going to give it up without a fight.

The day after he left Boonesborough, as the new village was named, the messenger met Henderson and his men with pack-horses loaded with all equipment necessary to build a town. The message was delivered and the pioneers hurried on regardless of the tales of horror they heard from panic-stricken settlers whom

they met on the trail fleeing from "the dark and bloody ground." On April 20, 1775, the pioneers reached Boonesborough just a little more than a month after Harrod and his friends had returned to their town.

It was spring, the trees were showing their tiny green leaves, and the flowers were blossoming everywhere. The settlers looked out over the landscape and found it a place of beauty. Forts and blockhouses were built without delay. The white men had taken the Indian hunting ground but they were not to hold it in peace for many years, for on all sides the Indians looked upon them with angry eyes and skulked in the forests or waited in ambush for some chance to put them out of the way.

On the Cumberland

Five years had gone by since Richard Henderson had made his purchase of land and there were yet no white men's cabins in the southern section bordering the Cumberland River. Though the Long Hunters had gone there and found game in abundance, the plains on which the buffalo ranged were still covered with dense cane thickets ten to twenty feet high. The only cleared spaces were around the salt licks, where elk, buffalo, and deer had tramped the vegetation with their ceaseless tracking.

Just as he had had to look for someone to lead settlers into the Shawnee country, so now Henderson had to seek a frontiersman to take the lead in settling the fertile regions of the Cumberland. Daniel Boone had spoken often of James Robertson, who had been such a force in the Watauga settlement and of whom the Indians said, "He has winning ways and never makes a fuss." Perhaps he would be willing to venture farther west! With Boone's help Henderson persuaded Robertson to do for the Cumberland country what he had done for Watauga.

Taking a scouting party of ten men, Robertson went westward along Boone's trail through the Cumberland Gap. Turning southward they traveled along a trail until they reached French Lick, now Nashville, Tennessee. This looked like good country. So they set to work building cabins, clearing land, and planting corn. When all the patches were planted, seven of the party returned to Watauga, leaving the three to keep the buffalo and Indians from the corn land and to protect the cabins.

When the seven returned to Watauga many families were ready to go into the venture with James Robertson, the man who had never failed them. It was agreed that most of the men should go overland, while others, with the women and children and the household goods, followed by boat down the Holston and Tennessee rivers into the Ohio and then up the Cumberland to French Lick.

The overland party left Watauga in October, 1779, taking only provisions for their immediate needs. While on the Wilderness Trail they met a party of adventurers on their way to Kentucky. After some persuasion on the part of Robertson, John Rains, the leader, consented to turn southward at the Cumberland and go with the Wataugans to the undeveloped land.

This band of two hundred or more pioneers was very different from the little group of seventeen families which Robertson had led over the Alleghenies nine years before. Even in this short period the mode of travel had changed and trails had widened, so that where pioneers had gone over the trail in Indian file they could now go three or four abreast.

Though they had a good trail as far as the Cumberland River, traveling by pack-horse in the winter of 1779–1780 was not easy. The weather was extremely cold, and the party was delayed by frosts and snow. Reaching the Cumberland River, they found it frozen over and they either had to risk driving their horses and cattle across the ice or turn back. They decided to go on, and just as they had got about half way across, the ice began to creak and groan. But it did not break, and they got safely over. Following the southward trail they reached French Lick Christmas Eve, 1779, tired, cold, and hungry but there was no time to lose in thinking about discomforts, for more land had to be cleared, more cabins built, and forts put up.

Some of the men rebelled at having to build forts, for they had seen no Indians on their way out. But Robertson, who was familiar with the habits of the red men, knew they would come as soon as the weather moderated and insisted that they fortify themselves without delay. Land was plentiful and the settlers scattered themselves over a large area, for they were permitted to locate anywhere within twenty-five miles of French Lick, which Robertson insisted should be the main settlement and have the largest fort. Nearly every week saw new families coming to the Cumberland and in less than a year the settlement boasted of eight stations or hamlets, the most distant of which was ten or twelve miles from Nashborough, the new name given to French Lick.

Busy as they were with their building, land clearing, and crop planting, the men who had come from Watauga could not help feeling anxious about their families who were to come by water. April came and they had not arrived nor had anything been heard from them. The men imagined all sorts of things that could have happened, for it was a dangerous road they were taking through the Chickamauga towns and the rapids of the Tennessee River.

Just as the anxious men had almost given up all hope of ever seeing their wives and children again, the little fleet came in sight, and there was much rejoicing at French Lick. As soon as all got settled everyone crowded around to hear the story of the river journey.

The Voyage of the "Adventure"

As soon as Robertson and the overland party had left Watauga preparations were made for making the boats which were to take the women and children to the new settlement. Poplar trees were cut down and hollowed out for canoes; planks were sawed for the flatboats which were boarded up and roofed, so that there would be some protection against the weather. In three months the fleet of thirty or more canoes, dugouts, and flatboats was ready.

On the morning of December 22, 1779, while the overland party was nearing the frozen Cumberland, the little fleet moved slowly out from Fort Patrick Henry (the present Kingsport), on the Holston River, led by Colonel Donelson's boat "Adventure," quite the largest and most imposing flatboat on the river. Following close upon the "Adventure" were the smaller boats and canoes grouped close together

so that messages could be passed from one to another.

Bringing up the rear of the fleet, but at some distance from the rest, was the flatboat of the Stewart family, some of whom had the smallpox. They were afraid to come in contact with the others lest they give them the dread disease, but they were anxious to go with the party to the Cumberland; so they agreed to follow at a distance, but close enough to get the camping signals.

Two months after they had left Fort Patrick Henry, the Wataugan fleet was joined by other boats going down the Tennessee River but expecting to go farther west when they reached the Ohio River. Each fleet was doubtless glad of the other's company, for the voyage lay through the country of the Chickamauga Indians, a band of renegade Creeks and Cherokees who had no love for the white men.

From the time they left Cloud's Creek the fleets endured hardship after hardship, for the river was filled with jutting rocks and islands, large and small. First one boat and then another got beached on the rocks, and much precious time was lost in getting them safely into the open current again. One of the boats was driven upon an island with such force that it sank, and the whole fleet had to go to the rescue. No lives were lost but the boat and cargo were badly damaged.

So many difficulties arose to slow them down that it was March before they had gone far on their journey and the wind and fog interfered with their progress. From the time they entered the Tennessee River until they left Muscle Shoals the Indians watched them from the shore, shooting at them as they passed slowly by. At the first Indian town the red men came out to meet them, pretending friendship. Being warned by a half-breed living in the Chickamauga towns that it was merely a trap to get them to land, the Wataugans increased their speed and got safely

by the village under the piloting of the half-breed.

At the next Indian town farther down the river they were not so fortunate. The main fleet had got by, but when the Indians saw the Stewart boat in the rear they took advantage of its helplessness, fell upon the passengers, and killed them all. Their punishment speedily followed, for some of the Indians got the smallpox and since they did not know how to treat this disease it spread throughout the villages and the red men died by hundreds.

Passing Lookout Mountain, the travelers left the Indian villages behind, but the bloodthirsty savages continued to follow along the cliffs above and shoot down upon the voyagers as they passed. In going through the Narrows at Lookout Mountain one of the canoes overturned, and the boat on which the Jennings family was traveling got separated from the fleet. The Indians were keeping up such a rapid fire from the cliffs above that the fleet could not wait for the lost boat, but it did halt long enough to rescue the overturned canoe and its crew.

A day or two later at four o'clock in the morning Mr. Jennings and his family saw the camp-fires of their party and called for help. Their boat was riddled with bullets and three of their passengers were missing. As they were going through the Narrows their boat had struck a rock, and the Indians, seeing them stranded, attacked them with all their force. Mr. Jennings, who had to give all of his attention to the Indians, told his son and two other men, one of whom was a Negro, to get out and push the boat off, but they got frightened and ran away, leaving the women to do the work.

Abandoning the shattered boat, the Jennings family were put on other boats, and the fleet embarked again upon its voyage. As they neared Muscle Shoals, the roaring of the rapids warned them of what was ahead. To take a fleet of thirty or more heavily laden boats through this whirling, swirling current, with sharp rocks jutting at many intervals, demanded courage of the highest type, a cool head, and a steady hand.

For three hours Colonel Donelson and his crew steered the way, and when they sailed into the quiet peaceful stretch of water beyond, with not a boat missing, all were ready to camp at the nearest spot and rest.

For two days all went well. Then one night while they were encamped on the river bank the dogs began to bark—a signal that Indians were near. Without waiting to investigate, all deserted the camp and rushed for the boats. In their haste they forgot their old Negro who was sleeping by the camp-fire. When they returned in the morning the Negro was still sleeping and there were no signs of Indians having been there.

By the middle of March the travelers were out of the Chickamauga country and were no longer annoyed by the savages, but they had been so long on the way that their food supply was getting low and the men were exhausted from constantly fighting off red men and steering boats through a rough current. All longed for their cabins on the Watauga, which they left three months before.

At the mouth of the Tennessee River the group broke up, one party going down the Ohio to the Mississippi River. From there some were going up the Mississippi to the Illinois country, and others down the same river to Natchez. The group which had set out for the Cumberland continued up the Ohio for four days. It was very difficult to paddle up the Ohio against the current for the river was high and the men were tired from their long journey. On the fifth day the fleet entered the Cumberland River, which was so small they feared they had lost their way and were on the wrong stream, but on they paddled and, as they went farther up, their courage was revived.

By the twenty-fourth of April they were at French Lick. For four months they had followed the river, through dangerous rapids and by hostile Indian towns. They had journeyed a thousand miles on four rivers—down the Holston into the Tennessee, up that winding stream into the Ohio and then up the Cumberland to the French Lick. Though their hearts were saddened by the loss of some of their party, there was much happiness on the Cumberland when the men sighted the good boat "Adventure" leading the little fleet into port.

Courage in the Wilderness

The families on the Cumberland had not been reunited very long when the Indians, angry at their having taken possession of the red men's hunting ground, began to annoy them. Scarcely a day passed that a settler was not shot from ambush or scalped

while hunting in the woods. No one went outside the gates of the fort alone. When water was needed, two went to the spring, one to watch for Indians while the other dipped up the water. In the fields the men worked in squads, back to back, so they could watch in all directions, or, if planting crops, a guard was stationed near by to protect the men and the horses as they worked.

Having to keep such diligent watch for the red men, the settlers could not get in much corn, and the little that was planted was hindered in its growth by the cold weather. The crops which survived the hard winter were damaged by the spring rains and swollen streams. Discouraged settlers left, the eight stations dwindled to two, and it seemed that the prophecy which Oconostota, the Cherokee, made would come true. At the time of the purchase of the land he said, "Brother, we have given you a fine land but you will have a hard time settling it."

As the Indians shot or scalped first one son or daughter, and then another, the pioneers wanted to abandon their new homes and return to Watauga, but Robertson encouraged them to stay on. They could not have gone far on the Wilderness Trail, for they had not even enough powder to defend their homes. When the supply of ammunition became alarmingly low, Robertson went with a party to their nearest neighbors at Harrodsburg, a distance of three hundred miles, for help. Their Kentucky friends at Harrodsburg were as generous as they dared be with their powder and bullets, but what they could spare was not enough. While Robertson returned to the Cumberland with their donation, the others went on to Boonesborough and Watauga for more.

When he went to Harrodsburg, Robertson left his family at Freeland's Station, which was connected with the Nashborough fort by a buffalo trail. So his first stop on his return was Freeland's. He was seen in the distance long before he reached the fort and the news of his arrival spread like wildfire. The supply of ammunition was at its lowest ebb, and now that relief had come the settlers felt secure.

As they sat around the fire that night Robertson

told them all the news he had heard of the outside world and the latest reports from the Revolution over the mountains. It was well into the night when they went to bed. They had scarcely had time to fall asleep when Robertson, who always slept with one ear open, heard the latch of the gate to the fort lifted. Seizing his rifle he whispered, "Indians!" and instantly every man was awake and on guard. Had Robertson not returned that day, the Indians probably would have massacred them all, for they had not enough powder in the fort to defend themselves.

The Choctaws, Creeks, and Cherokees continued to kill and scalp, sometimes wiping out whole families at one time. Again the cry arose to desert this new land which had brought them only trouble and go back to Watauga, but Robertson, even though his own son had been killed by the red men, again persuaded them to stay. He assured them that if they returned they would have to fight their way through, for the angry Indians were all about them and as many dangers lurked in the homeward path as were around them at the fort. So with true pioneer courage they held on to their homes.

Part VII
THE COLONIES REVOLT

15
The Indians in the Revolution

WHILE THE WESTERNERS were clearing the wilderness and making their homes over the Blue Wall, their kinsmen on the Atlantic seaboard were getting deeper and deeper into a quarrel with the mother country across the seas.

As the settlements grew in size and in number, it was natural that there should be problems which could not be solved by a government three thousand miles away, across a vast ocean. So the colonists were forced to manage their own affairs, and became more and more independent and self-reliant.

For ten years the British Parliament passed acts which the colonists thought were not fair, and for ten years they protested against them. At last the quarrel between the thirteen colonies and Great Britain broke out into open warfare.

One month after the Wataugans and Richard

Henderson had made the treaties with the Indians at Sycamore Shoals, the first shot of the American Revolution was fired at Lexington in Massachusetts. Though the frontiersmen had heard only vague rumors of the quarrel, when the break came they were in sympathy with their parent colonies. There were fewer than a thousand of them and they could not hope to contribute much in either soldiers or money, but they were eager to help. In August, 1775, four months after the war began, the western settlements were organized for military service, and the riflemen were ready to go where and when they were needed to aid their Atlantic neighbors.

On the Warpath

In a country where many thousands of acres of land were claimed and owned by Indians a war could not be fought without taking them into consideration. The settlers did not care to draw the Indians into the fight, for they knew that theirs was not the white man's method of warfare. So they urged the red men to stay out of it and keep to themselves.

The officers of King George, however, saw how the Indians could be of great service to the royal army, for they knew the country and the trails to the settlements. If the savages could be persuaded to attack the frontier villages, the western riflemen would have to protect their homes and so could not aid the eastern armies.

The red-coated soldiers of the King were commanded to give "talks" to the Indian warriors, offering them guns, ammunition, and blankets. But, best of all, they promised that the King's army would drive the settlers from the Indian hunting ground. The Indians were much puzzled! What should they do? Had not the white settlers told them they must obey King George, who was their father? Had they not been told that their Father-over-the-Water owned all the white man's land and would protect the Indians from their enemies? Now these same white men were fighting the soldiers of the Great Father and saying the land was theirs. Who were right, the redcoats or the settlers who were taking their land? The "talks" of the King's soldiers were stronger than the arguments of the traders and settlers, even the most friendly ones .

George Rogers Clark

North of the Ohio, the man who fought the redskins and the redcoats most successfully was George Rogers Clark. This famous Virginian was born in sight of the Blue Ridge, not far from Jefferson's home, Monticello. Like Jefferson, he often looked at the beautiful Blue Wall of the mountains and wondered what lay beyond. When he was nineteen years old, he went on a surveying and exploring expedition and saw the country west of the mountains. He finally took up some land on the upper Ohio River and built a cabin there. But the spirit of adventure lured him on, and in 1773 he locked the door of his cabin and went with a party of Virginians into Kentucky. During the next year he fought the Indians south of the Ohio, and while he was protecting the settlers of Kentucky, he fell in love with the beautiful region and decided to settle there.

When the settlers in Kentucky needed help from Virginia, Clark traveled seven hundred miles, mostly on foot, to Williamsburg, and persuaded the Virginia legislature to extend protection to the Kentucky settlements beyond the mountains.

Meantime the American Revolution had begun, and the Indians all along the frontiers were attacking the American settlers. Tomahawks flashed and log cabins went up in flames, as the terrible Indian war-whoop shook the hearts of courageous frontiersmen.

Clark saw that if the Americans were to hold the Great Valley, these Indian raids would have to be stopped, and this meant defeating the British, who now held all the forts that had once belonged to the French. He therefore went again to Williamsburg, and got permission from Governor Patrick Henry

to raise some troops for an expedition. Soon he had about a hundred and fifty men, mostly Virginians, and started with them down the Ohio. When he reached the falls of the Ohio, he camped and organized his little army, which had now been increased by the frontiersmen who had willingly joined his expedition.

Their first objective was Kaskaskia, and Clark and his men floated down the Ohio until they passed the mouth of the Tennessee River. Then they went overland on foot, carrying their heavy guns and ammunition, through a region of swamps and prairie, until they sighted the village of Kaskaskia. They came up to it so quietly in the dark that they captured it without firing a gun. The villagers and the English soldiers were having a dance, when suddenly they saw Clark standing, with his arms folded, in the doorway. "Go on with your dancing," said Clark, "but remember that now you are dancing under Virginia's flag and not England's."

When General Hamilton at Detroit heard that Clark had captured Kaskaskia, he sallied forth to stop this young Virginian. He marched to Vincennes (called Fort Sackville by the British) and occupied it.

Hamilton had been supplying the Indians with arms and ammunition, and the red men, who fought in their own way, took many scalps of whites and

enemy Indians to Hamilton at Detroit. They called Hamilton the "Hair Buyer."

Clark knew that Hamilton would next march upon Kaskaskia. He said, "We must either quit this country or attack Mr. Hamilton. No time is to be lost." He had only a few hundred men and not enough supplies, but there was not time to get help from faraway Virginia. In February he began his march. It was bitterly cold. The men had no tents. There had been heavy rains, and the prairies were under water. Part of the way, they had to cross the "Drowned Lands." They camped on a hillock at night. The little drummer boy amused them by floating part of the way on his drum. On they went, the water often breast-high, until they came in sight of Vincennes. Here the British felt safe because of the heavy rains and the flooded lowlands. They did not know the spirit of Clark and his gallant little army. Hamilton surrendered, and thus Clark won the Illinois country and helped to win the whole Northwest Territory for the new United States of America.

Nancy Ward, "Beloved Woman" of the Cherokees

South of the Ohio, too, the warriors dug up the war hatchet, put on their sinister war paint, made fresh bows and arrows and new moccasins, ready to start on the warpath. Shawnee chiefs from the west and chiefs from the Chickamauga and Creek towns from the south met in a council of war with the Cherokees of North Carolina and Georgia in the Cherokee council house. Together they plotted against the settlers and planned raids by which to drive them from their homes. No village on the frontier from Georgia to Virginia was to escape the Indian torch and tomahawk.

Near the council fire in her accustomed place sat Nancy Ward, the Beloved Woman of the Cherokees. Many times had she shown her loyalty to her white friends and had saved first one and then another from the tortures of her warriors. Listening closely to the talks of the Indian chiefs, she missed no word of the plots being hatched by her own people against the pale-faces.

At her first opportunity Nancy Ward got word to Isaac Thomas, a trader in the village. She told him of the plans of the Cherokees to send war parties against the Watauga villages under the leadership of their highest chiefs, Old Abraham, Raven, and Dragging Canoe, and urged him to warn his people.

Thomas called in his fellow traders, Fallin and Williams, and told them all that Nancy had said. The three messengers, starting out by different routes, arrived at Watauga the same day. Warnings were sent to all the distant and near-by cabins, commanding the settlers to hasten to the forts at Watauga and at Heaton's (Eaton's) Station, which lay between the two forks of the Holston River.

The roads to the stockaded villages were thronged with men, women, and children, carrying what household goods they could and driving their cattle, for no one knew how long the siege might last. One settler, Mrs. Bean, refused to leave her cabin, such was her confidence in her red friends, but she was soon to find that Indians on the warpath are very different from Indians in peace time.

Safe within the forts, the settlers could do nothing but wait and listen for the war-whoop of the red enemies or perhaps a bird call, which would mean their signal of attack. In less than two weeks from the time of their councils at Chota, the Cherokees were on the warpath determined to do their part in ridding the Indian hunting ground of the white enemy.

Four War Parties

While Dragging Canoe, the most dreaded Cherokee chief, with his warriors, hideous in their war paint, crept through the forests toward Heaton's (Eaton's) Station, Colonel Thompson of Virginia with five companies of riflemen hastened to the aid of the valley settlements. Arriving at Heaton's Station the latter part of July, he waited at the fort for a report from the scouts he had sent out. When they came in, reporting several hundred Indians on their way to the fort, Colonel Thompson and his army decided to go toward Long Island and meet them.

As they marched through the forests, they came upon Dragging Canoe and his advance guard lying in ambush. The soldiers fired upon them so suddenly and so unexpectedly that the Cherokees fled, terrified. The riflemen, believing all was over for the day, started back to the fort to warn the settlers to be ready for the attack. Dragging Canoe, seeing the men turn back, thought they were retreating and immediately gave his war-whoop. Brandishing his tomahawk he shouted to his warriors, "The Unacas are running. Come on and scalp them." But the Unacas, or white men, were not running away. Instantly they turned upon the pursuing foe and in ten minutes had killed so many of them that the rest fled, carrying Dragging Canoe, who had been badly wounded.

In that ten minutes Lieutenant Moore, an American soldier, had a hand-to-hand battle with an Indian warrior, whom he had wounded. The angry savage rushed upon him with his tomahawk raised ready to strike, but the lieutenant, with the swiftness of one accustomed to Indian warfare, drew his knife and struck at the raised hand. Grasping the knife by the blade the Cherokee held it fast, the steel sinking deeper and deeper into his flesh. Moore with his free hand gave his hatchet a swing and with one blow sent the young warrior to his death.

With the retreat of Dragging Canoe and his scouts, one settlement was saved from the ravages of the Indians, and one of the Cherokee plans to drive out the settlers failed.

While Dragging Canoe was making his unsuccessful attack upon Heaton's Station, sly and crafty Old Abraham of Chilhowee was marching with his warriors along the Nolichucky Path at the foot of the mountains to Watauga. As he went through the valley in which he had planned to kill and burn with-

out mercy, he found every cabin save one deserted. In that one lingered Mrs. Bean.

So sure was Old Abraham that the white people had but recently fled that he sent Mrs. Bean to his camp on the Nolichucky River and hurried his warriors on, expecting every minute to come upon the unhappy families fleeing from him. In his haste he neglected to burn the cabins and destroy the crops as he had agreed at the council of war to do.

As the sun rose, the war party arrived at Watauga, just in time to see the women slip cautiously through the stockade gates into the open. For ten days or more the Wataugans had been shut up in the fort. Hearing of the defeat of Dragging Canoe at Heaton's Station and seeing no signs of Indians, the women, believing the danger was over, were going out to milk the cows. Scarcely had the gates shut behind them when from the forests rose the blood-curdling war cry of Old Abraham. Terrified, the women dashed wildly back for the gates, the Indians in close pursuit.

All made the enclosure except Bonnie Kate Sherrill, a dark-haired maiden, brave and swift-footed. With quick thought she leaped for the stockade wall. As she climbed up, Nolichucky Jack, the Indian fighter, shot her pursuer and with his free arm lifted her over the wall to the safety of the fort.

Colonel James Robertson and John Sevier with their forty or fifty men lost no time in turning their guns upon Old Abraham's war party. As fast as the women could mold the bullets, the men loaded and fired their muskets. Old Abraham, seeing he was no match for these American soldiers fighting for the safety of their families, withdrew his warriors to the surrounding forests, where they skulked and watched, hoping someone would come out after them.

Colonel Robertson gave orders that no one was to leave the enclosure without his permission. Unfortunately, two boys, Cooper and Moore, anxious to finish repairing a cabin, slipped unseen through the gate to get some wood. As they reached the creek a short distance from the fort, the Indians fell upon them. Their screams, which were heard at the fort, brought no assistance, for Colonel Robertson, not knowing anyone had left the stockade, thought it only a trick of the Indians to get the soldiers out and would not let anyone leave. Cooper, thinking he could swim the creek, jumped in, but the water was too shallow and the Indian arrows flew at him so fast he could not escape and was killed. But Moore was less fortunate, for his captors took him to their village, where they tortured and burned him. After skulking around the fort for twenty days, the Indians went back to their villages. The second plan of the Cherokees to destroy the white settlements had failed.

While Old Abraham and his warriors were annoying the Wataugans, Mrs. Bean awaited her fate at Old Abraham's camp on the Nolichucky. When the scheming chief returned, he plied her with questions concerning conditions at the fort, to all of which she replied that the settlers were well able to defend themselves. Old Abraham, unable to make up his mind whether to return her to her people or kill her, kept her captive and she spent her time teaching her red sisters to make butter and cheese.

When he decided that it was best to kill her, Old Abraham had all preparations made to burn her. Mrs. Bean gave up all hope then of ever seeing her family again but was determined to show no fear. Just as the Indian brave was about to touch the torch to the

leaves heaped about her, Nancy Ward, the white man's friend, came to the rescue and demanded her release. No one dared to disobey the Beloved Woman; so Mrs. Bean was soon on her way to Watauga.

Raven, a daring and intelligent Cherokee warrior, had been sent to lay waste the Carter's Valley settlements. Hearing of the defeat of Dragging Canoe and Old Abraham and finding the settlers prepared to defend themselves, he moved on without even molesting them. But the war parties that went to drive the white men from Clinch Valley were more successful. Meeting with no opposition, they destroyed crops, homes, and villages and took captive men, women, and children.

While the Cherokees were attacking the back settlements of Virginia and North Carolina, the southern frontiers of South Carolina and Georgia suffered a like fate at the hands of the Creeks and Chickamaugas. The British plan of banding together the Indians against the western settlements was partly successful.

Retaliation

The settlers saw that there could be no peace on the frontier until the Indians were subdued. Though they were expecting the British enemy at any time, the four southern colonies organized expeditions with as many men as they could spare to go against the

Cherokees in the Lower, Middle, and Overhill towns.

While Colonel Samuel Jack of Georgia and Colonel Andrew Williamson of South Carolina destroyed the Lower towns, Colonel Rutherford of North Carolina led his army of two thousand men over the Blue Ridge Mountains to the villages of the Middle Cherokees. Driving before them the cattle which were to furnish meat while they were on the campaign, and leading their pack-horses loaded with other provisions, the soldiers went through the Swannanoa Gap below Watauga and crossed the French Broad River. Wherever they went they found that the Indians had left their villages, but they carried on their work of destruction just the same, determined to put an end to the Indian attacks which had destroyed the white settlements since the beginning of the war with Great Britain.

When he had burned the Middle towns, Colonel Rutherford decided to go on to the valley towns. Taking only half of his men, he started over the mountains, but he could not find the pass through which he could lead his army and he was forced to turn back. It was fortunate for him that he lost his way, for at the gap through which he should have gone, a band of Cherokee warriors was waiting to attack him.

As soon as the Wataugans were sure the Indians

had left the forest surrounding their villages, they organized their forces to meet Colonel William Christian, who was coming from Virginia to lead the expedition against the Overhill Cherokees. Eighteen hundred men armed with knives, rifles, and tomahawks gathered at Great Island on the Holston to carry war into the unexplored regions of the mountain Cherokees. While camping at Lick Creek eight miles from Great Island, Alexander Harlin, the scout whom Colonel Christian had sent out, brought in the report that three thousand Cherokees were waiting for the white men at the French Broad River and boasting that the white army should never cross the river. But the western fighters, ever mindful of the Indian outrages on their homes, were not to be frightened off.

Led by Isaac Thomas, a trader, who knew the mountain towns better than anyone else, the American soldiers and riflemen hurried on, examining carefully every sign of camps but finding no Indians. Just before they reached the French Broad, a Tory trader came to their camp bearing a flag of truce. Though Colonel Christian knew he was a spy from the enemy's camp, he gave orders that he was to have the freedom of the place. After looking around as much as he wished, the trader returned to the Cherokees.

Reaching the French Broad River Colonel Christian and his soldiers pitched camp as if they planned to stay several days; but as soon as it grew dark a large part of the army was sent down the river with orders to cross over and in the morning to come up the other side. The next morning the rest of the force crossed over, but there were no Indians in sight. After drying out their baggage, which had got wet in the stream, the soldiers started again on the march, listening and watching on all sides lest the Indians be concealed in ambush along the way.

Meanwhile the Tory trader had returned to the Indian camp at Great Island, where the warriors had assembled to defend the entrance to their country and drive back their white neighbors. Hearing his report that the white man's army was as numerous as the trees in the forest, the Cherokees lost courage, and when Starr, a white trader in their towns, advised them against attempting to oppose the white men, the warriors abandoned the Island and went back to their mountain homes.

Colonel Christian, finding the Island deserted, took possession and made it the base of all his maneuvers in the Indian villages. From there he and his soldiers went out and destroyed all the villages of the enemy Indians, but the friendly towns were spared. Chota, the village of Nancy Ward, was not molested; but

Tuskagee, the town in which Samuel Moore had been tortured and burned, was completely wiped out.

The Indians, seeing that they were helpless against these white soldiers and realizing they had more to fear from them than from the redcoats of King George, sued for peace. In July, 1777, at Great Island on the Holston, a peace treaty by which "peace should forever exist between them" was signed by all of the Cherokee chiefs except Dragging Canoe, who refused to accept peace on any terms.

Gathering about him the most lawless of the young Cherokee braves, he went to the towns of the Chickamauga Indians on the Tennessee River about thirty-five miles below the present Chattanooga. Hidden in the wooded ravines of the Cumberland Mountains about the narrow gorge of the Tennessee River, Dragging Canoe sent out foraging parties against the frontiers of Georgia and the Carolinas at frequent intervals for more than a year. Finally Colonel Evan Shelby decided to invade the Chickamauga country and destroy Dragging Canoe and his villages, in which had gathered not only renegade warriors of several Indian tribes but bandit white men as well.

The soldiers were notified to meet at Big Creek, where trees were to be felled and canoes made in which the army would go down the Holston River into the Tennessee, and then on to the Indian villages. The canoes completed, the soldiers paddled silently down the Tennessee, and so completely surprised the Chickamaugas in their stronghold that they fled without even fighting. But Shelby and the westerners were relentless in their purpose and followed in pursuit. Towns were burned, crops destroyed, and fleeing warriors killed. When their work of destruction was finished, the soldiers sank their canoes and returned home through the mountains.

The red men were vanquished, their country was made desolate, and the western settlements were free from Indian attacks for a time. Peace did not last long, however. As soon as the Chickamaugas had rallied from the onslaught of the white army, they persuaded the Cherokees to break their peace treaty, and Indian raids began again and continued until peace was made between Great Britain and the thirteen colonies, and the British redcoats were withdrawn from the Valley.

16

Western Riflemen

THE BRITISH IN THE SOUTH

DURING THE FIRST YEARS of the American Revolution, most of the fighting was in the North, but when the British came into Savannah in December, 1778, the fighting was transferred to the southern colonies. Up to this time, the chief concern of the colonists who lived over the Blue Wall had been the Indian attacks on their settlements. But when the British soldiers began to overrun Georgia and South Carolina, the western riflemen found that they had two things to do—protect their own frontier and aid the American armies.

Some of the people in the western Carolinas, as in the other colonies, still sided with the British. These were called Tories, and when the British troops came into the region, the Tories aided them. But most of the frontiersmen fought against England, because they believed that the English were stirring up the Indians to attack the American settlements, and because for many years the English government had tried to prevent the American colonists from settling west of the mountains.

By the summer of 1780, the British had forced South Carolina and Georgia to submit to British rule and were rapidly making their way into North Carolina, scattering the patriots and forcing their armies to disband. Cornwallis took up his headquarters in Charlotte, North Carolina, and sent Colonel Ferguson, one of his best officers, toward the mountains, to gather the Tories together and break up the American patriot camps wherever he found them. Ferguson was an excellent soldier and an expert rifle shot, and he assembled about a thousand Tories, in addition to his small band of regulars.

Meantime, Colonel Charles McDowell, in command of the North Carolina militia, became certain that Ferguson intended to attack the Americans, and he sent a call to the western settlements for as many riflemen as they could spare. Mustering over two hundred men each, John Sevier and Isaac Shelby hurried over the mountains, and engaged in several skirmishes with the British. The best thing that they did was to capture Fort Anderson, on the Pacolet River, where Captain Patrick Moore, a noted Tory, was in command.

In this western warfare, sometimes the British were successful and sometimes the American riflemen, but when the British won the important battle of Camden, the Americans almost gave up. Colonel McDowell retreated across the mountains, and Ferguson followed him as far as Gilbert Town, about seventy miles from Charlotte. There he stopped and sent a haughty message to the American officers west of the mountains telling them that if they did not yield, he would march into their country to burn their homes and destroy their fields.

This was too much for Shelby and Sevier to endure. They determined to raise as large a force of riflemen as they could and stop Ferguson. Colonel William Campbell of Virginia soon joined them, with his troops.

The Battle of Kings Mountain

They all met at Sycamore Shoals on the Watauga River on September 25, and began their march across the mountains on the next morning. On the 29th, Colonel McDowell joined them, and other officers and men came to them as they marched. It is said that in this company were "three thousand settlers from the extreme backwoods, rough, half-civilized men whom no labour could tire, and whose rifles seldom missed their mark."

When Ferguson heard of the advance of this determined band, he sent a call to Cornwallis for more troops, and then took up his stand on Kings Mountain. This is a lofty ridge, about thirteen miles long and so narrow that "a man standing on it may be shot from either side." Ferguson felt that from this mountain top he could hold off any number of foes. He did not know the mountain men of the western frontier.

When the riflemen learned where Ferguson was, they made a night march in the rain. They were unprotected even by hunting shirts, which they had taken off and wrapped around their gun locks to keep them dry. The next morning they planned their attack. In the afternoon of the same day, they reached the foot of the mountain, divided into three columns, and began their march upward from different points, with orders to push ahead until they met at the top.

Ferguson, feeling secure on his lofty perch, was completely surprised. The British were brave and fought desperately, but what could they do against enemies who fought like Indians, from behind trees? The mountain slopes were covered with forests, and the riflemen had perfect cover as they advanced.

Twice the redcoats raised the white flag, and twice Ferguson cut it down, crying that he would "never surrender to such a set of banditti" as the mountain men. Not until the brave Ferguson had fallen, fatally wounded, did the British surrender to the westerners. Taking their prisoners and spoils of war, the riflemen filed down the mountain and joined the rest of the army. Their work done, they hastened back over the mountains to their homes.

The Americans were much encouraged by the victory of Kings Mountain. They felt that it was the turning point in the struggle, and they gained fresh hope and courage. For Cornwallis, it was the beginning of the end, and he hastily withdrew into South Carolina.

Meanwhile, Washington sent General Nathanael Greene to take command of the southern army in North Carolina. This splendid soldier organized the scattered, untrained patriots into a gallant fighting force, and, from then on, he "lost every battle [including the famous Battle of Guilford Court House] and won every campaign."

In the end, Cornwallis proclaimed an empty victory in North Carolina and withdrew to Virginia, where, shortly after, he surrendered to the American commander-in-chief, George Washington.

In 1783 a treaty was signed between Great Britain and the United States, which ended the Revolutionary War. The United States of America was now an independent nation, and this young nation was soon to be tested as to its ability to handle its own affairs.

Part VIII
THE SPANISH ON THE BORDER

17

Spanish Red Men

AT THE END of the Revolution the western boundary of these United States was the Mississippi River, and the southern boundary was a line a little north of the present state of Florida. South of this line and west of the Mississippi was the region claimed by the King of Spain. Thus Spain owned the mouth of the Mississippi River and could control its traffic.

The Valley was being rapidly settled by soldiers coming to claim the sections of land given them for their military services during the Revolution, and Spain began to fear these grasping backwoodsmen, who could live on so little and endure such hardships. She feared that they would seize her possessions in the South and West. Something must be done to keep them from getting farther into the Valley.

Spain now had almost complete control of the Creek, Choctaw, and Chickamauga Indians. By uniting them against the Americans, she might drive the latter from the Valley, thus protecting her own frontiers against the Americans and at the same time keep for herself the valuable Indian trade. If this plan failed, she might close the Mississippi River to American traffic, thus bottling up the products of the rich Valley and so discourage the backwoodsmen that they would be forced to seek homes elsewhere.

The Spaniards and the Indians

In carrying out plans for destroying the settlements in the Valley, particularly those on the Cumberland and in Kentucky, the Spanish governor found an excellent ally and agent in Alexander McGillivray, the "white leader" of the Creek Indians. McGillivray's father was Lachlan McGillivray, a Scotch trader, and his mother was Sehoy, a Creek princess. He returned to his people after he had been educated in the white man's schools. With the clear-headedness of the Scotch and the cunning of the savage, he had a tremendous influence over his people and was made their chief. The Spanish minister to the United States, Don Diego de Gardoqui, knew how powerful McGillivray was and made an alliance with him at Pensacola, Florida. According to their agreement, McGillivray was to unite the Creeks, Choctaws, and Chickamaugas against the western settlements and so direct the raids against them that the white men would get worn out with the uncertainty of the attacks and leave the Valley.

The westerners had not yet recovered from the Indian outrages of the Revolution, and now they were forced to defend themselves against new attacks. Knowing that the British had withdrawn from the Valley, they could not understand why the Indians should still trouble them. When it was suggested that Spain might be responsible, the frontiersmen did not like to believe it, for Spain had always seemed friendly.

The westerners were forbidden by the central government in far-away Philadelphia to carry war into the Indian territory. The Indians went out in small groups, killed, scalped, and robbed, and then returned to their villages, knowing that the white men would not pursue them. Neither Creeks, Choctaws, nor Chickamaugas would take the blame for these raids. Spain, while pretending friendship with the Americans, encouraged the attacks and provided the guns and ammunition, all the while claiming that the real reason for the Indian hostility was that the settlers were continuing to encroach upon their lands, which was, of course, partly true.

For more than ten years the western frontiersmen fought off the frequent attacks of the red men. If they had acted together in open warfare, they could have ended the contest, but they were forced to carry on a defensive warfare only, and they could do little but watch and wait. Scarcely a day passed that a settler was not killed; sometimes whole families were wiped out and their cabins burned; but the backwoodsmen stood their ground and would not be driven from their homes.

The Boy Who Came Back

In May, 1788, Colonel James Brown with his wife and nine children started west to take up the grant of land which had been given the colonel for his services during the Revolution. From their home in North Carolina they went over the mountains into the Holston Valley, and there built a boat which would take them to the Cumberland by the river road—the same route the early settlers of the Cumberland had taken in the "Adventure" down the Holston into the Tennessee and on to the Nashville settlement by way of the Ohio and Cumberland rivers.

On the fifth day of the journey they came in sight of the villages of the Chickamauga Indians, the most savage red men of the south. Hidden in the ravines and caves along the Tennessee River where it forces its way through the Cumberland Mountains, these redskins felt secure from the white men, and so were daring in their attacks upon the river voyagers.

As the boat neared Tuskigagee Island Town, chief Cutleotoy and three of his warriors went out to meet it. After a friendly visit with Colonel Brown, they returned to their village, and the boat moved on, its passengers rejoicing that the Indians were peaceable. Cutleotoy and the warriors had no sooner reached their village than they sent messengers to the towns down the river to tell the warriors to meet Colonel Brown's boat and capture it.

Four canoes with forty warriors stopped Colonel Brown's boat under the pretense of wanting to trade with him, and Brown, not wishing to offend them, allowed them to come on board. While the forty warriors were inspecting the boat, eighty other canoes came up and the Brown family was surrounded with Indians, who pillaged the boat and killed the men. The colonel himself was killed and thrown overboard. Mrs. Brown, the four daughters, and young Joseph were spared but were taken captives to the Indian villages.

Young Joseph, then a lad, was given to an old white man, named Tunbridge, who was ordered to take him to Nickajack Town, the village from which Cutleotoy had come that morning. As Tunbridge entered

the town with his little captive, a great tumult arose. An ancient squaw hurried up and, brandishing a club, said, "You must kill him. He is old enough to know and see things. He will get back to his people and return with an army and kill us all. You must kill him." But Tunbridge shut the lad up in his own house and refused to let the squaw have him.

Joseph understood not a word, but he knew from their voices that they were angry and that he was the cause of the quarrel. Tunbridge protected him as long as he could, but when Cutleotoy came and demanded that Joseph be given up, he had to surrender the boy. Leading him out toward the village named Running Water, where he could be tortured and killed without interference from white people, the Indians planned a great dance and feast. On the way, however, fear got the better of Cutleotoy, and he decreed that neither he nor his men could kill the little white boy, for after all he was the prisoner of their head warrior whom they greatly feared. So Joseph was taken back to Nickajack Town, where he was adopted into the family of the chief. Dressed like an Indian boy, he worked in the fields, learned the games of his Indian brothers, and lived and looked like an Indian lad. As he worked and played, he listened to their talks, watched their actions, and learned everything about them he could.

At the end of a year and a half, word came to the Nickajack Town that John Sevier, "Nolichucky Jack," the dreaded white warrior, had invaded the towns on the Coosa River and was on his way to the Chickamauga villages to demand the release of every white man, woman, and child there. In a few days the rumor proved true. The red men fled, and Joseph was returned to his mother, and all went back with Nolichucky Jack to the safety of the settlements. Part of the old squaw's prophecy had come true.

Five years later the rest of it was to be fulfilled. Worn out with the constant and unending attacks on the Cumberland and Kentucky settlements, the westerners at last determined to invade the Chickamauga towns. Joseph Brown, now a grown young man, remembered enough about his captivity to lead the

attacking expedition. Soldiers and riflemen from Kentucky, Cumberland, Holston, and Watauga met at Nashville, and from there they struck a southward trail.

Several days later they reached the banks of the Tennessee River some time during the night, and, concealing themselves in the bushes, they waited until dawn. As soon as it was light enough to see their way, the frontiersmen crossed over. Some made rafts of cane, but the more impatient ones swam across, led by Joseph Brown, who was the first to reach the opposite bank.

Near the river was Nickajack Town, where Joseph had been a captive for almost two years, and the frontiersmen were in the center of the town before the Indians knew they were anywhere near their hiding place. Surprised and panic-stricken, the savages made for the canoes at the river bank, but most of them were killed or captured on the way.

When Joseph appeared before the prisoners, they were filled with horror, for they recognized him as the boy whose father and brothers they had killed in this same village five years before. The old squaw could only murmur, "I said he would come back and kill us all." The two towns, Nickajack and Running Water, were burned to ashes, and there was peace on the western frontier. Spain had failed in her first plan to drive the Americans from the Valley.

18

Spanish Intrigues

SINCE THE BEGINNING of time, rivers have played an important part in the history of the land of the western waters. The Indians used them as roads between their villages. After the explorations of La Salle, the Mississippi River became the highway for French canoes carrying furs between the northern trading posts in the Illinois country and the southern posts at New Orleans. As the woods rangers went farther inland, other rivers, the Ohio, the Cumberland, and the Tennessee, became the roads to the Alabama forts of the French.

SPAIN HOLDS THE GREAT RIVER

The English settlers who came into the western valleys followed the Watauga, Holston, and Clinch rivers. Kasper Mansker made one of the first trips in a flat-boat down the Tennessee and Mississippi rivers to Natchez. The Mississippi was to play an even greater part in the history of the valley.

The westerners beyond the Blue Wall had three outlets for their trade. They could go by pack-horse eastward through the forests and over the mountain trails to the trading posts at Fort Moore or Fort Congaree or other forts on the fall line of the rivers, and float their furs down these rivers to the Atlantic seaports and ship them abroad. Or they could go northward to the Great Lakes, by which they could reach the St. Lawrence River and float down to the sea, and from there ship their furs abroad. Or they could go southward, down the Mississippi to New Orleans, and ship their furs to the markets of the Atlantic states, the West Indies, or Europe. The last way was by far the easiest, but Spain now owned the port of New Orleans and therefore controlled the navigation of the Great River.

Spain saw here a chance to accomplish what she had failed to do when she tried to stir up Indian raids against the settlers. She could close the Mississippi to the westerners and force them to leave the Valley or to swear allegiance to the King of Spain.

Spain therefore forbade the western settlers to ship their produce down the river, and when some of the more bold or daring pioneers risked sending shiploads of tobacco, hemp, and other products, their property was seized and sold.

In 1788, when Estevan Miró became governor, the

river was opened up to the use of the settlers, but the Americans had to pay such high duty on their products that commerce in that direction was almost impossible. They appealed to their new Congress to make a treaty with Spain allowing them the free use of the Mississippi, but Congress was slow to act because there was much jealousy between the Atlantic states and the country west of the mountains. The congressmen from the Atlantic states were opposed to the settling of the West and were willing to do everything to prevent it. The Mississippi Valley, with its fertile soil and vast natural resources, was growing much too rapidly for them. Even those who favored the western settlements thought that the frontiersmen should ship their products over the mountains to the eastern coast towns. This was George Washington's belief at that time. He thought that nothing would tie the western country to the East so strongly as trade back and forth between them, and, as president of the United States, he wished for a strong union of all the people, both eastern and western.

Most of the southern states fought for the free navigation of the Mississippi because many of them owned land upon it. Thus there was much difference of opinion in the central government.

When, through the recommendations of John Jay, a treaty was about to be signed by which the states would give up the use of the river for twenty or twenty-five years, the western people were alarmed and angry, especially those in the Kentucky and Cumberland settlements, who felt that their very life depended on the Great River.

This discontent again gave Spain a good chance to try to win the settlers away from the United States. Intrigue now took the place of force. Spain sent her secret agents to talk to the discontented westerners and persuade them that the only thing for them to do was to swear allegiance to Spain and thereby gain the free navigation of the river and be able to sell their products in all the markets of the world.

Among the secret agents was General James Wilkinson, an officer in the army during the Revolution, who lived in Kentucky. He was a smooth talker, and the westerners believed in him because of his position during the war. He constantly reminded them that Congress was not interested in them, and he found many people who welcomed the thought of an alliance with Spain. But fortunately there were others who were not willing to give up to Spain the independence which they had just won so hardly from Great Britain. They were farsighted enough to see that Spain could not always hold Florida and the western territories against this growing group of independent Americans.

Finally Congress awakened to the real meaning of the situation, and in 1795, twelve years after the close of the Revolution, signed the Pinckney Treaty, by which the West got free navigation of the Mississippi River. From that time, the Valley grew in population and in trade.

THOMAS JEFFERSON LOOKS BEYOND THE BLUE WALL

The English in the Great Valley could now ship their goods by way of the Mississippi River, but as long as Spain held New Orleans, the river was really controlled by a foreign country. The man who, more than anyone else, finally won the mouth of the Mississippi for the Americans was Thomas Jefferson. This great Virginian was born within sight of the Blue Ridge. He did not follow wilderness trails, as Washington did, but from his beautiful home at Monticello, high in the Virginia hills, he looked out toward the Blue Wall and realized the future greatness of America.

As governor of Virginia, as member of Congress, as member of Washington's cabinet, and as president of the United States, he did everything he could to encourage the exploration of the West. He sent Lewis and Clark to the Pacific coast, and Pike to the Rockies. He helped John Jacob Astor establish a fur-trading post at the mouth of the Columbia River, clear across the continent.

When Spain was threatening to bottle up the Mississippi Valley by forbidding Americans to use the port of New Orleans, Jefferson watched matters closely and with the greatest anxiety. Then Spain transferred most of her American lands to France. France was an even more dangerous enemy than Spain, for the great Napoleon was in power and dreamed of a vast colonial empire in America, as La Salle had done over a hundred years before.

Therefore, when the United States had a chance to buy from France, not only the port of New Orleans but also the great region of Louisiana west of the Mississippi, Jefferson, who was then president, acted promptly, and at last, by the Louisiana Purchase of 1803, the United States gained complete control of the Father of Waters, into which all the western waters flow.

For two centuries and a half the Great Valley had been the scene of struggles and conflicts between savages and white men and between rival nations. Spain, France, and England—all had been forced to yield to the vigorous young nation.

Little by little the Indians had been pushed from their hunting grounds. As the white men advanced, the villages of the red men had been destroyed. Forests and streams now served the home-seekers. Lands not won by strategy or conquest were acquired by purchase. The eastern part of the Great Valley, which, at one time or another, had been Spanish, French, English, became, in the first years of the nineteenth century, a part of the United States of America.

INDEX

Index

ACHTAHACHI, Choctaw chief, 21, 22, 145
Adair, James, English trader, writes to Prieber, 127-28; quoted, 144, 145; life of among the Indians, 155-56, 161-65; important book on Indians written by, 156
"Adventure" (Donelson's boat), building of, 25; voyage of, to the Cumberland region, 25-56; 296
Agents, French, 122, 130, 178, 187
Agents, secret, sent by Spain to the Cumberland region, 305
Alabama, De Soto in, 20-25, 107; Chickasaws in, 100 ff.; Cherokees in, 116; Prieber in, 129; Creeks in, 135 ff. *See also* Fort Toulouse; Fort Louis; Mobile
Alabama River, 171
Albany, N. Y., 49
Allegheny Mountains, 223, 242, 248
Allegheny region, 116
Allegheny River, vii, 174, 183, 185
Alligators, 67
American Indians, history of, 156
American Revolution, 175, 219, 240, 259, 263-89, 293, 295, 296, 305, 306; Indians in, 264-84
"America's bloodiest battle," 23-24, 107

Ammunition, 109, 111, 125, 143, 187, 197, 218, 219, 258, 265, 268, 295
Animals, habits of, 209; *See* name of animal, as Bear
Ani-yun-wiya, 116
Apalache, 7, 8, 16, 17
Apalachee Bay, 6
Apalache village, 7
Appalachian Mountains, vii, 20, 82, 116
Apples, wild, 20
Appomattox Indians, 78, 79, 80
Appomattox River, 175
Arkansas, De Soto in, 30
Arkansas Indians, 44
Arkansas River, 44
Arquebuses, 16
Artaguette, Pierre d', attacks the Chickasaw Indians, 110-13
Arthur, Gabriel, leaves Fort Henry, 78-80; in the Cherokee country, 83-93; at Port Royal, 88; captured by the Shawnee Indians, 90; at Saura, 92; returns to Fort Henry, 92-93; 116, 153, 175, 176, 242
Astor, John Jacob, 306
Atta Kulla Kulla (Ouconecau). *See* Little Carpenter
"At the fall of the leaf," 93, 157
Augusta, Ga., Cofitachiqui near, 18; junction of trading paths, 176; Oglethorpe in, 180

BABIES, double-jointed (dolls), 157
Backwoodsmen, 231, 232, 233, 293, 294, 296
Bacon, a hunter, 214
Ball play, 119, 137, 139, 147, 233
Barbecues, at Sevier's home, 240
Barges, 28, 30
Bartram, William, 137
Battle of Bloody Marsh, 182
Battle of Camden, 287
Battle of Guilford Court House, 289
Battle of Kanawha, 237
Battle of Kings Mountain, 287-89
Battle of Mauvila. *See* "America's bloodiest battle"
Batts, Captain Thomas, 79
"Bay of the Cross," 6
"Bay of the Horses," 10
Beads, 44, 46, 89, 118, 146, 153, 156
Bean, Captain William, first settler in Tennessee, 224-26
Bean, Mrs. William, 224-27; refuses to go to the Watauga fort, 271; captured by Old Abraham, 275; at Old Abraham's camp, 275; rescued by Nancy Ward, 277
Beans, 30, 66, 84, 104, 119, 196
Bear, 66, 160, 203, 205, 209
Bear meat, 120, 210
Bear-skins. *See* Skins
Bear's oil, 84, 118
Beaufort, S. C., 88
Beautiful River. *See* Ohio River
Beaver, 90, 91, 104
Beaver-skins. *See* Skins
Beds. *See* Furniture, Indian
Beds, feather, 205
"Beloved Woman" of the Cherokees. *See* Ward, Nancy
Benches. *See* Furniture, Indian
Bienville, Sieur de, 107-11; attacks the Chickasaw Indians, 112-15; 171, 172, 173
Big Creek, 283
Biloxi Bay, 107
Bimini, Island of, Ponce de León hears of, 4
Blackberries, 104
"Black drink," 118
Blacksmiths, 12, 52
Blacksmith shops, 190
Black Warrior River, 172
Blankets, 27, 31, 46, 103, 147, 226, 230, 233, 234, 237, 265
Bledsoe, Anthony, 214
Bledsoe Lick, 214, 220
Blockhouses, 246
Bloodhounds, 13, 16
Bloody Marsh, Battle of. *See* Battle of Bloody Marsh
Blue Ridge Mountains, 94, 95, 265, 280, 306
Blue Wall, vii, 75, 78, 81, 82, 83, 86, 93, 95, 99, 107, 116, 175, 177, 183, 186, 187, 191, 263, 265, 285, 303, 306
Bluffs, Chickasaw. *See* Chickasaw Bluffs
Boats, French, captured by the Cherokee Indians, 125; plundered by the Chickasaw Indians, 109
Bogs, *See* Swamps
Boisbriant, Pierre, 173
Bonnefoy, Antoine, 125-26
Bonnie Kate Sherrill. *See* Sherrill, Bonnie Kate
Boone, Daniel, with Gen'l Braddock, 186; in Kentucky, 215-19; singing in the cane-brake, 216; escapes from the Indians, 218; 224, 225, 226; cuts the Wilderness Trail, 243-44; 247
Boone, Squire, 216, 218, 219
Boonesborough, founding of, 243-44; 246, 258
Boone's Creek, 224
Boone's trail, 247
Boundaries, 231, 293
Braddock, General Edward, 186
Bridge, raccoon, 160
Brobdingnags (in *Gulliver's Travels*), 208

INDEX 313

Brown, Colonel James, starts west, 296-97
Brown, Jacob, settles in the Nolichucky Valley, 231
Brown, Joseph, captive in the Chickamauga towns, 297-99
Buckskin, 205. *See also* Deer-skins
Buffalo, 41, 66, 105, 160, 203, 205, 209-10, 216, 221, 246, 247
Buffalo country, 64
Buffalo meat, 120, 207, 209
Buffalo trail, 258
Bull, Lieutenant-Governor William, of South Carolina, 196-97
Bullet mould, 213
Bullet pouch, 205, 226
Bullets, 143, 156, 190, 244, 254, 258, 276
Bunks. *See* Furniture, Indian
"Bushy Head" (Captain John Stuart), 197

CABEZA DE VACA, 7, 10-11
Cabins, building of, 206, 220, 224-25, 230, 231, 232, 242, 244, 247, 249
Cahokia, French mission, 173-74
Calumet, 42, 43
Camden, Battle of. *See* Battle of Camden
Cameron, Alexander, superintendent of Indian affairs, 232
Campbell, Colonel William, 287
Canada, 37, 39, 40, 49, 69, 75, 106
Cane-brakes, 203, 212, 215, 219, 221
Cannon, 53, 190; brought over the mountains, 191-93; at Fort Loudoun, 196-99
Caravans, traders', 157, 158, 159, 160, 161. *See also* Pack-trains
Carolinas, the, 37, 79, 106, 113, 134, 169, 283, 285. *See also* North Carolina; South Carolina
Carpenters, 12, 52, 58
Carter, John, settles in Carter's Valley, 230-31
Carter's Valley, 230, 231, 232, 279

Catawba Indians, 176
Cattle, 5, 162, 196, 228, 248, 271, 280
Cavalcade, 93
Cavaliers, 12
Cave-people, the Cherokees, 116
Céloron, 114, 115
Charleston, S. C., trading paths to and from, 108, 117, 140, 153, 168-69, 176; Prieber's connection with, 127, 128, 129; Cherokee chiefs go to, 194. *See also* South Carolina
Charleville, French trader, 155
Charlotte, N. C., Cornwallis at, 286, 287
Charlotte Harbor, Florida, 13 note
Chattahoochee River, 136, 180
Chattanooga, Tennessee, 283
Chatuga, 126
Cherokee capital. *See* Chota
Cherokee country, 80, 91, 92, 117, 129, 130, 131, 133, 143, 153, 169, 172, 212
Cherokee Indians, 81, 82, 84, 85, 86, 87, 88, 89, 90, 92, 99, 100, 109, 116-34; legend of, 116; dress of, 118; at home, 118; on the trail, 118; houses of, 118, 120; games of, 119; rank of, in council meetings, 120; in London, 121-25; capture French traders, 125; 127, 135, 136, 140, 154, 155, 172, 174, 176, 177, 180, 187, 188, 189, 191, 193, 195, 199, 204, 232, 233, 235, 252, 259, 270, 272, 280, 281, 284
Cherokee nation, 134, 169, 176, 187; Crown of the. *See* "Crown of the Cherokee Nation."
Cherokee Prime Minister. *See* Prieber, Christian Gottlieb
Cherokee towns, 122, 131, 132, 155, 158, 178, 187, 198
Cherokee trading path, 177
Cherokee villages, 83-84, 91, 116, 117, 127, 133

Cherokee war, 187, 195-99, 212, 223
Cherokee warriors, 83, 91, 92, 117, 120, 122-25, 131, 132, 133, 233
Chicago River, 63
Chickamauga country, 255, 283
Chickamauga Indians, 144, 252, 279, 283, 284, 293, 294, 295, 296
Chickamauga towns, 250, 252, 270, 283, 299
Chickasaw Bluffs, 27, 102, 110, 170; Second Chickasaw Bluff, 64; Fourth Chickasaw Bluff, 114
Chickasaw country, 25-27, 104, 106, 108, 109, 111, 156, 158
Chickasaw houses; summer house, how made, 102; winter house, how made, 102, 103; store-house, how made, 102
Chickasaw Indians, 26; visited by De Soto, 28; teach Spanish how to trap rabbits, 30; 64, 99; legend of, 100-1; location of country, 100-1; how they lived, 102-5; French expeditions against, 108-15; 125, 127, 133, 135, 140, 144, 145, 146, 148, 154, 164, 171, 172, 173, 180
Chickasaws' river, 101, 109
Chickasaw towns, 110, 146, 148, 149
Chickasaw villages, 102, 105, 106, 110, 112, 113
Chickasaw warriors, 105, 110, 112
Chilhowee, village of Old Abraham, 273
China, route to, 39, 46, 47, 48
Choctaw country, 164, 172
Choctaw Indians, 99, 100, 101, 108, 110, 113, 114; description of, 145; how they flattened their heads, 146; called "wolf cubs," 147; sports of, 147; vanity of, 147; not trusted by the French, 148; 154, 165, 172, 173, 176, 180, 259, 293, 294, 295

Choctaw nation, 106
Choctaw towns, 146
Choctaw warriors, 112, 147, 148, 165
Chota, Cherokee capital, 131, 132, 133, 188, 197, 234, 235, 272, 282
Christian, Colonel William, leads expedition against the Cherokee Indians, 281-82
Christmas Day, 63, 88, 89, 184, 237, 249
Christmas Eve, 249
Chunky, 119, 139, 147
Chunky ground, 137
Chunky stone, 119
Chunky yard, 119, 137
Clark, George Rogers, 175; in the Revolution, 265-70
Clarksville, Virginia, 79
Clay, in building, 102, 120, 136
Clinch River, 230, 302
Clinch Valley, war parties in, 279
Cloud's Creek, 252
Coça, 20, 21
Cofitachiqui, Indian princess, visits De Soto's camp, 18; gives presents to De Soto, 19-20; made captive by De Soto, 19; escapes from De Soto's army, 20
Cofitachiqui, Indian village, 18, 24
Colbert, Jean Baptiste, 39
Collars, iron. See Slave collars
Colts, how handled by the packhorsemen, 158
Columbia, S. C., Fort Congaree near, 176
Columbus, Christopher, 3
Congaree River, 176
Congaree trail, 177
Contests, Indian, 119-20, 139
Cooper, James, killed by the Indians, 276
Coosa River, 20, 136, 141, 172, 299
Corn, parched, 226, 238

INDEX 315

Cornwallis, Lord, headquarters of, at Charlotte, N. C., 286; asked for troops by Ferguson, 288; surrenders, 289
Council Bend, Mississippi, 27
Council fires, Indian, 120, 137, 270
Council houses, Indian, 139; Cherokee, 120, 137, 270; Creek, 136
Council of war, Indian, 270, 275
Coureurs de bois. See Runners-of-the-woods
Coweta Town, 180
Coytmore, Lieutenant, killed by Oconostota, 195
Creek boys, training of, 138
Creek country, 169, 176
Creek Indians, 99, 100, 108, 109; two divisions of, 136; houses of, 136-37; games of, 137; women of, 139-40; 141-46; 154, 176; in England, 177-78; 180, 204, 252, 259, 279, 293, 294, 295. *See also* French Creeks
Creek towns, 142, 146, 270
Creek villages, 135
Creek warriors, 136, 138, 139, 142, 143
Crossbows, 16, 28
"Crown of the Cherokee Nation," presented to King George, 124
Cuba, 6, 8, 13, 19, 30
Cumberland, Maryland, 186
Cumberland country, 247
Cumberland Gap, 212, 216, 247
Cumberland Mountains, 242, 243, 283, 296
Cumberland River, 213, 220, 240, 243, 246, 247, 248, 250, 256, 258, 294, 296, 302
Cumberland settlement, 249, 251, 258, 299, 301, 305
Cumings, Sir Alexander, 122-25, 177
Cutleotoy, Chickamauga Indian chief, 297-99

DANCES, Indian, 22, 23, 84
"Dark and bloody ground," 218, 246
D'Artaguette, Pierre. *See* Artaguette, Pierre d'
"Debatable land," 178, 180
De Brahm, John William Gerard, engineer at Fort Loudoun, 192
Deer, 41, 66, 81, 105, 164, 203, 205, 206, 210, 215, 246
Deer-skins. *See* Skins
De León, Juan Ponce. *See* Ponce de León, Juan
Demeré, Captain Raymond, at Fort Loudoun, 189, 197-98
De Mombreun, Timothy, 220-21
De Soto, Hernando, expedition of, 12-33; sails for Florida, 13; lands at Tampa Bay, 13; finds Ortiz, 13, 14; treatment of Indians, 16, 17, 19, 21, 22; and Cofitachiqui, 17-20; and Achtahachi, 21-24; at Mauvila, 22-24; in the Chickasaw country, 25-27; finds the Mississippi River, 27; death and burial of, 31; 37, 66, 107, 116, 145, 148
Detroit, Michigan, 268, 269
De Vaca. *See* Cabeza de Vaca
Diamonds, 94
Dinwiddie, Robert, Governor of Virginia, 174, 184, 185
Dogherty, Cornelius, trader, 155
Dogwood thicket, Town in, 17, 19
Dolls. *See* Babies
Doña Isabel. *See* Isabel, Doña
Donelson, Colonel John, 250, 252-55
"Double-jointed babies" (dolls), 157
Dragging Canoe, 271-73, 275, 279; 283
Drake, a hunter, 214
Drake's Pond, 214
"Drowned lands," 269
Ducks, wild, 66

Dunmore, John Murray, Earl of, Governor of Virginia, 237
Dunmore's War, 237

EATON'S STATION. *See* Heaton's Station
Elk, 105, 203, 209, 246
Elk "gardens," 209
Elk meat, 210
Elk-skins. *See* Skins
Elvas, the gentleman of, 13, 20, 22
"English Chickasaw, the." *See* Adair, James
English Chickasaws, 143
English Creeks, 141, 142
English forts. *See* names of forts, as Fort Henry
English settlements. *See* Settlements, English
English traders. *See* Traders, English
Eno, Indian village, 82
Erie, Lake, 53

FAIRFAX, Lord, 183
Fallam, Robert, 79
Fallin, trader, sent to warn Watauga, 271
Father-over-the-Water, George II, King of England, 194; George III, 265
Feasts, Indian, 22, 43, 84, 120
Feeding places (of animals), 209, 210
Ferguson, Colonel, at Kings Mountain, 286-88
Findley, John, 216, 218
Finley. *See* Findley
"Fire-water," 161, 162
Flatboat, 250
"Flatheads." *See* Choctaw Indians
Florida, discovery of, 4; naming of, 5; De Soto in, 12-17, 31, 33; Spanish settlements in, 37; Gabriel Arthur in, 87-88; Spanish military posts in, 168;

and the fur trade, 176; relations of with Georgia and South Carolina, 176-83; at the end of the Revolution, 293
Flutes, sign of peace, 23
Fontaine, John, 94
Food, Indian, 104, 120, 121
Forbes, General John, 186, 193
Forbes's Road, 186
Forks of the Ohio, 174, 186, 193
Fort Anderson (English), 286
Fort Assumption (French), 114, 173
Fort Charles (English), 175
Fort Chartres (French), 173
Fort Congaree (English), 176, 303
Fort Crèvecoeur (French), 57, 58, 170
Fort Cumberland (English), 186
Fort Duquesne (French), 174, 186, 187, 193
Fort Frederica (English), 181
Fort Frontenac (French), 45, 49, 50, 51, 52, 53, 54, 55, 57, 58, 170
Fort Henry (English), English leave from, 78, 80; Colonel Wood commander of, 79; Needham returns to, 84, 85; Cherokees at, 91-93; Arthur returns to, 92; at head of navigation, 175; on Occoneechee Trading Path, 176
Fort Le Boeuf (French), 174, 183
Fort Loudoun (Loudon), building of by the English, 191-93; siege of, 195-97; 198, 199
Fort Louis (Mobile; French), 107, 171
Fort Machault (French), 174, 183
Fort Massac (French), 175
Fort Miami (St. Joseph; French), 56, 58, 61, 63, 170
Fort Mobile. *See* Fort Louis
Fort Moore (English), 176, 177, 303
Fort Necessity (English), 186

Fort New Orleans (French), 107, 171
Fort Niagara (French), 53, 58, 170
Fort Patrick Henry (English), 250, 251
Fort Pitt (English), 187. *See also* Fort Duquesne
Fort Prince George (English), 188, 194, 195, 196, 197, 198
Fort Prudhomme (French), 66, 69, 168, 170
Fort Rosalie (French), 108, 171
Fort Sackville (English), 175, 268. *See also* Fort Vincennes
Fort St. Joseph. *See* Fort Miami
Fort St. Louis (French), in the Illinois country, 69, 107, 170; on Matagorda Bay, 171
Fort St. Simon (English), 182
Fort Stanwix (English), Treaty of, 223
Fort Tombigbee (French), 172, 173
Fort Toulouse (French), 129, 131, 133, 141, 172
Fort Vincennes (French), 174, 220, 268, 269. *See also* Fort Sackville
Fountain of Youth, 4, 6
Fourth Chickasaw Bluff. *See* Chickasaw Bluffs
Fox, Lieutenant, tries to arrest Prieber, 129
Fox River, 41
Franciscans, 55
Franklin, Benjamin, 241
Franklin, State of, 241
Franklinites, 241. *See also* Wataugans
Frederica, Georgia, 129, 130, 181, 182
Freeland's Station, 258
French and Indian war, 54, 174, 175, 185, 187, 188, 193
French Broad River, 280, 281
French Choctaws, 149
French claims, 67, 115
French Creeks, 141, 142, 143

French forts. *See* names of forts, as Fort Prudhomme
French Indians, 132, 134, 148, 171, 177, 178, 185, 187, 190, 213
French John, 132, 133, 134
French Lick (Nashborough, Nashville), 155, 220, 247, 248, 249, 250, 256
French missions. *See* Missions, French
French settlements. *See* Settlements, French
French traders. *See* Traders, French
Friars, 5, 12, 16, 55
Frontenac, Count, Governor of Canada, 39, 49, 50, 53, 63, 68
Frontenac. *See* Fort Frontenac
Frontiers. *See* Indian attacks
Frontiersmen, viii, 223, 244, 247, 264, 266, 268, 285, 295, 301, 304
Frontier villages, Indian attacks on, 264, 266; raids upon planned by Cherokee Indians, 270
Fruit, dried, 30, 66
Fruits. *See* names of fruits, as Apple
Fur-bearing animals. *See* names of animals, as Bear. *See also* Skins
Furniture, Indian, beds, 103, 121; benches, 121; bunks, 103; seats, 103, 137
Furs, 45, 46, 47, 49, 50, 52, 53, 54, 84, 100, 103, 106, 107, 153, 154, 155, 162, 172, 204, 206, 302, 303. *See also* Skins
Fur trade, 46, 47, 50, 107, 141, 153, 154, 155, 169, 170, 172, 173, 175, 176, 178, 302. *See also* Skins

GAME, 38, 55, 75, 101, 104, 121, 139, 146, 157, 203, 204, 210, 223, 225, 228, 246
Games, Indian, 119, 139, 299

INDEX

Gardens, vegetable, 119, 139, 156, 162
Gardoqui, Don Diego de, Spanish minister to the U. S., 294
Garrisons, at Fort Frontenac, 50; at Fort Loudoun, 194, 196
Gentleman of Elvas, the. *See* Elvas, the Gentleman of
George II, King of England, 100, 121, 122, 123, 124, 180, 192, 194
George III, King of England, 223, 264, 265, 283
Georgia, Cherokees in, 116, 270; Prieber in, 129; Creeks in, 135; Great Mortar in, 143-44; as a frontier colony (the Debatable Land), 177 ff.; defended by Oglethorpe from Spanish attacks, 181-83; attacked by Indians, 279-80; in the Revolution, 285-86. *See also* Augusta; Savannah
Germanna, home of Governor Spotswood, 94
Giant hunter. *See* Spencer, Thomas Sharp
Gilbert Town, Colonel Ferguson at, 287
Gist, Christopher, 184, 185
Glen, Governor James, of South Carolina, 187, 188, 189
Gold Hats, Land of, 3-33, 145
"Golden Horseshoe, Knights of." *See* "Knights of the Golden Horseshoe"
Grant, Ludovick, tries to arrest Prieber, 128
Grapes, wild, 20, 203
Great Father, George II, King of England, 192; George III, 265
Great Island on the Holston, 281, 282; treaty at, 283
Great King - over - the - Water, George II, King of England, visit of Cherokees to, 121-25
Great Lakes, 37, 45, 46, 49, 52, 54, 107, 173, 303
Great Meadows, 186
Great Mortar, Creek chief, 140-44
Great River. *See* Mississippi River
Great Spirit, Chickasaws obey, 100-1
Great Tellico, 126, 127, 128, 131, 132, 134
Great Valley. *See* Mississippi Valley
"Great Warrior," highest title of the Cherokees, 117, 118
Green Bay, 41, 52, 54, 61, 62
Greene, General Nathanael, in the Revolution, 289
"Griffon," La Salle's ship, 53, 54, 55, 56, 57, 58, 170
Guaxula, town of the Cherokees visited by De Soto, 20
Guides, Indian, 7, 13, 15, 16, 17, 41, 79, 80, 148, 180, 198
Guilford Court House, Battle of. *See* Battle of Guilford Court House
Gulf of Mexico. *See* Mexico, Gulf of
Gun Merchant, Creek warrior, 142
Gunpowder, 46, 113, 130, 143, 146, 157, 218, 219, 227, 258, 259
Guns, 46, 55, 64, 87, 90, 109, 110, 111, 143, 148, 153, 154, 156, 166, 171, 172, 185, 191, 192, 193, 196, 197, 199, 207, 219, 227, 232, 234, 265, 268, 295

"HAIR BUYER" (General Henry Hamilton), 269
Half-King, Indian chief, 184
Hamilton, General Henry, at Vincennes, defeated by George Rogers Clark, 268-70
Handsome Fellow, Creek warrior, 142
Harlin, Alexander, scout with Colonel Christian, 281
Harmon, Matthew, long hunter, 215

Harrod, James, goes to Cumberland, 242-43, 246
Harrodsburg, 242, 243, 258
Hasecoll. *See* Indian John
Hatchets, 44, 90, 153, 154, 156, 193, 212, 226
Havana, Cuba, 182
Heads, flattening of, 145-46
Heaton's Station, 271, 272, 273, 275
Helmets, of gold, 11
Hemp, 303
Henderson, Richard, 243, 244, 246, 247, 263-64
Hennepin, Father, 54, 55
Henry, Patrick, Governor of Virginia, 266, 268
Hickory, 103, 114
Hides. *See* Skins
Highlanders, 181, 182
Highways, 47, 101, 121, 125, 154, 210, 302
Hinges, wooden, 225
History of the American Indians, The, by James Adair, 156
Hiwassee River, vii
Hogs, 13, 16, 18, 20, 27, 162
Holliday, a hunter, Spencer shares knife with, 220
Holston River, 212, 223, 224, 230, 242, 247, 250, 256, 271, 283, 296, 301, 302
Holston Valley, 296
Home building, 230, 247. *See also* Cabins, building of
Homemakers, Creeks as, 139
Home-seekers, 228, 230
Homes, pioneer, 225, 230. *See also* Cabins, building of
Honeycut, neighbor to William Bean, 227
Honey-locust, 102
Horse, banqueted by Indians, 84
Horse-bells, 157
Horse paths, 232
Horse races, 233, 240
Horseshoes, golden, 94
Horton, Joshua, long hunter, 213

Hospitality, Indian, 18, 19, 25, 40, 42, 43, 44, 66, 84
Hostages, 194
Houses, Indian, 102-3, 118, 120, 136-37
Huneycut. *See* Honeycut
Hunters, 55, 64, 81, 146, 192, 203-22; how they dressed, 205-6; how they lived, 205-8
Hunter-woodsmen, 205
Hunting camps, 203, 207
Hunting grounds, Indian, vii, 169, 203, 204, 210, 212, 232, 242, 246, 256, 265, 272, 307
Hunting knives. *See* Knives
Huron, Lake, 54

IBERVILLE, Sieur d', 106, 107, 108, 171
Illinois Country, La Salle in, 57 ff.; French traders in, 108, 125, 302; French soldiers in, 110; hunters and settlers in, 213, 255; George Rogers Clark in, 266-70. *See also* Starved Rock
Illinois Indians, 42, 43, 56, 57, 58, 59, 61, 63, 69, 107, 170, 173
Illinois River, 56, 58, 59, 61, 63, 69, 107, 170
India, short route to, 3
Indiana. *See* Vincennes; Illinois Country; Marquette; La Salle
Indian attacks on frontiers, 95, 193, 194, 242, 256-58, 281, 293
Indian John, 80, 81, 82, 84, 85, 86
"Indian night," 26
Indian raids. *See* Indian attacks
Indians. *See* names of Indian nations, as Cherokee Indians
Indian trade. *See* Fur trade
Indian warfare. *See* Warfare, Indian
Indian women, work of, 139, 140
Iron collars. *See* Slave collars
Iroquois Indians, in Canada, 46, 49; attack the Illinois Indians, 58-59, 170; capture Tonty, 61-62

Isabel, Doña, wife of De Soto, 13

JACK, Colonel Samuel, leads expedition against the Cherokees, 280
James River, 175
Jamie, negro slave, with Joshua Horton, 213
Japan, route to, 46
Jay, John, and the navigation of the Mississippi River, 304
Jefferson, Thomas, 265, 306-7
Jenkins, Robert, cause of War of Jenkins' Ear, 180-83
Jennings family, on the "Adventure," 254
Jesuit Relations, 38, 41, 47
Jesuits, 40, 45, 46
Joliet, Louis, 39-44, 45, 49, 51, 54, 78
Judd's Friend (Judge's Friend). See Outacite
Jumonville, Joseph Coulon de, French officer, 186

KAHOKIA. See Cahokia
Kanawha, Battle of. See Battle of Kanawha
Kankakee River, 56, 59, 63
Kaskaskia, 173, 175, 268, 269
Kentuckee, 216
Kentucky, Daniel Boone in, 208, 218; Thomas Sharp Spencer from, 219-20; and Treaty of Fort Stanwix, 223; on the Wilderness trail to, 244, 248; settlers in, 258, 299; George Rogers Clark in, 266; and the Spaniards, 294; joins in attack on Chickamaugas, 300-1; importance of Mississippi River to, 305
Keowee, Cherokee town, 177, 188
Ketagustah, Cherokee warrior, 124

Kings Mountain, Battle of. See Battle of Kings Mountain
Kingsport, Tennessee, 212, 250
Knights, with De Soto, 12
"Knights of the Golden Horseshoe," 93, 94
Knives, 44, 46, 89, 90, 121, 143, 153, 154, 156, 198, 205, 213, 220, 224, 226, 228, 281
Knox, James, long hunter, 210, 212

LA CHINE, La Salle's trading post near Montreal, 46, 47, 48
Lacrosse, 119
Lances, Spanish weapons, 16, 27
Land grants, 264, 296
Land of Gold Hats. See Gold Hats, land of
Land of the western waters. See Western waters, land of
Land purchases, 243
Lantagnac, Chevalier de, 133
La Salle, Sieur de, 45-71; dreams of a New France, 45; at La Chine, 46; in the Ohio country, 48; at Fort Frontenac, 50; searches for the Mississippi River, 53-63; claims the New World for France, 67; attempts to establish colony, 69-71; death of, 71; mentioned, 102, 106, 168, 169, 170, 171, 302, 307
Laurel, 82, 203
Laws in Watauga, 231, 232
Lead mines, 173
"Lean-to," of hunters, how made, 206
Legends, of Chickasaw Indians, 100-1; of Cherokee Indians, 116
León, Juan Ponce de. See Ponce de León
Lewis, Major, builds Virginia fort, 188, 189
Lexington, Massachussetts, 264
Lick Creek, 281
Licks, discovered by hunters, 214
Linsey (linsey-woolsey), 205

INDEX 321

Little Carpenter (Ouconecau), in London, 123; promise of, 125; friendly to English, 131, 188-189; with General Forbes, 193; tries to prevent war, 194-95; loyal to Captain Stuart, 198-99
Little Tennessee River, 117, 192
Long Hunters, 210-22, 223, 246
Long Island, now Kingsport, Tennessee, 212, 272
Looking glasses, 156, 157. See also Mirrors
Lookout Mountain, 253, 254
Lord Dunmore's War, 237
Loudoun, John Campbell, Earl of, fort named for, 192
Louis XIV, King of France, 50, 67, 68
Louis XV, King of France, 173
Louisiana (Mississippi Valley), claimed by La Salle for France, 68; defended from English, 107; French forts in, 171; bought by the United States, 307. See also New Orleans
Louisiana Purchase, 307
Louisville, Kentucky, 34
Lower Cherokees. See Cherokee Indians
Lower Creeks. See Creek Indians
Lower towns, Cherokee, 117, 188; expedition against, 280
Lower towns, Creek, location of, 136, 141
Lulbegrud Creek, the naming of, 208
"Lynn" tree (linden), 213
Lyttelton, William Henry, Governor of South Carolina, 194, 195

MABILE. See Mauvila
McDowell, Colonel Charles, in the Revolution, 286-87
McGillivray, Alexander, "white leader" of the Creeks, 294
McGillivray, Lachlan, 294
Mackinac, Strait of, 54

Maize, 19
"Man who got lost, the." See Prudhomme, Pierre
"Man with the Iron Hand, the." See Tonty, Henri de
Mankiller, Cherokee Indian, 131, 132, 133, 134
Mansker, Kasper, long hunter, 214, 215, 219, 302
Mansker's Lick, 214
Marquette, Father Jacques, 39-44, 45, 49, 51, 54, 78
Massachussetts, 264
Matagorda Bay, 171
Mattock, 225, 230
Maul, 225, 230
Mauvila, 22, 23, 107
Meat, jerked, 205, 207; smoked, 40
Medicine, frontier, 163-64, 213
Membré, Father, 66, 69
Memphis, Tennessee, 27 n, 114, 173
Men, Indian, work of, 139
Mermaid Tavern, Cherokee Indians at, 124
Mexico, 10, 11, 19
Mexico, Gulf of, 38, 51, 67, 68
Miami country, 56
Miami Indians, 69
Miami River, 55, 56
Michel, Jean, 69
Michigan, Lake, 41, 55, 61, 62, 78, 170
Michilimackinac, 62, 69
Michilimackinac, Straits of, 40, 52, 54
Middle towns, Cherokee, 117; expedition against, 280
Middle towns, Creek, 141
Military service, land grants for, 264, 296
Mills Creek, Maryland, 186
Mink, 157
Miró, Estevan, Spanish governor, 303-4
Mirrors, 153, 156. See also Looking glasses

Missionaries, 154; Sulpitian, 48; Jesuit, 37, 106-7, 109, 172; Franciscan, 55. See also names of missionaries, as Hennepin
Missions, French, 78, 173
Mississippi, De Soto in, 25, 27 n; Choctaws in, 146. See also Natchez
Mississippi River, vii, viii, 27, 30, 31, 33, 38, 39, 41, 43, 44, 45, 47, 48, 51, 52, 53, 56, 57, 59, 63, 64, 66, 67, 69, 71, 75, 78, 99, 100, 101, 106, 107, 109, 110, 114, 115, 125, 146, 153, 168, 169, 170, 171, 173, 214, 255, 293, 294, 302; navigation of, controlled by the Spanish, 303-7; treaties concerning, 304-5, 306
Mississippi Valley, 37, 49, 51, 68, 69, 78, 99, 107, 108, 115, 153, 154, 155, 156, 164, 168, 169, 171, 173, 174, 175, 176, 177, 187, 214, 220, 266, 284, 293, 294, 295, 301, 303, 304, 306, 307, 308
Missouri, De Soto in, 30
Missouri River, 43, 64
Mobile, Alabama, 107, 113, 131, 154, 173
Mobile Bay, 22
Mocozo Indian chief, Ortiz befriended by, 15
Mohegan Indian hunter, La Salle's, 55, 57
Mohetans, 89
Monongahela River, vii, 174, 199
Monticello, Virginia, home of Jefferson, 265, 306
Montreal, 45, 46, 47, 58, 63
Moore, Colonel Patrick, at Fort Anderson, 286
Moore, Lieutenant, fights with Indian warrior, 273
Moore, Samuel, captured by the Indians, 276, 283
Moscoso, Luis de, 31
Moss, elk feed upon, 209; used for bandages, 213
"Mossing places" of elk, 209

Mountain Cherokees. See Cherokee Indians
Moytoy, Cherokee emperor, 127, 128
Mulberries, 104
Mulberry trees, 67
Muscle Shoals, 252, 254
Musgrove, Mary, and Oglethorpe, 178
Muskets, 68, 113, 276. See also Guns
Muskrat, 157

NAPOLEON, and the Mississippi Valley, 307
Narrows, The, in the Tennessee River, 254
Narvaez, Pánfilo de, expedition of, 6-10
Nashborough, 249, 258. See also French Lick; Nashville
Nashville, Tennessee, 155, 247, 296, 301. See also French Lick; Nashborough
Natchez, Mississippi, Fort Rosalie near, 108, as village and trading post, 171-72, 214, 255, 302
Natchez Indians, 108, 110, 154, 158, 163, 171
Needham, James, 78-86; at Fort Henry, 78; goes over the Blue Wall, 82; in the Cherokee village, 83-84; killed by Indian John, 86; mentioned, 91, 93, 116, 153, 175, 176
Needham and Arthur expedition, 78-93
Neely, Alexander, 208
New Orleans, founding of, 107, 171; French trade in, 108, 125, 154, 302; in the hands of Spain, 303, 306; acquired by the United States, 307
Niagara. See Fort Niagara
Niagara River, 170
Nickajack Town, 297, 299; expedition against, 301
Nika, La Salle's guide, 55, 57

INDEX 323

"Niña," ship of Columbus, 3
Nolichucky Jack. *See* Sevier, John
Nolichucky Path, 273
Nolichucky River, 231, 240, 242, 275, 277
Nolichucky settlement, 231
Nolichucky Valley, 231
North Carolina, Occoneechee Trading Path through, 82; part of Cherokee country, 116; grateful to Oglethorpe, 183; hunters in, 204; westward migration from, 226-27, 231-32, 296; attitude of Wataugans toward, 240-41; Richard Henderson of, 243; Cherokees of, 270; Indian attacks on frontiers of, 279; in the Revolution, 286-89
North Holston Valley, 224
Northwest Territory, 270

OCCONEECHEE Indians, 78, 80, 81, 82, 85, 86, 91, 92
Occoneechee Island, 79, 81, 86
Occoneechee Trading Path, 78, 80, 93, 176
Occoneechee village, 85, 91
Ochese Creek (Ocmulgee River), 135
Ochese Creek Indians. *See* Creek Indians
Ocklockonee Bay, 10
Ocmulgee River, 135
Oconostota, Cherokee warrior, at Fort Prince George, 194-95, 198-99; prophecy of, 257-58
Oglethorpe, James, 177-83; takes Indians to England, 177; and Tomo-chici, 177; in the Debatable Land, 178; and Mary Musgrove, 178; wins the friendship of the Creeks, 178-80; and the Spanish, 181-83
Ohio River, vii, viii, 43, 48, 64, 116, 125, 174, 175, 187, 203, 243, 248, 252, 255, 256, 265, 266, 268, 270, 296, 302

Ohio Valley, 173
Old Abraham, Cherokee warrior, 271, 273-79
Old Hop, Cherokee warrior, 131, 132, 133, 134, 187, 188-89, 192
Old Rabbit, Cherokee Indian, 123
Ontario, Lake, 45, 49, 170
Opossums, 207
Orient, route to, 44, 46, 75
Ortiz, Juan, 13-15, 30
Ottawa River, 47
Otter, 157
Ouconecau. *See* Little Carpenter
Outacite, Judge's friend, 194
Overhill Cherokees. *See* Cherokee Indians
Overhill towns, Cherokee, 117, 192; expedition against, 280
Overhill villages, Cherokee, 126, 192. *See* Overhill towns
Overland journeys, 57, 61, 78, 247-48
Ox, wild (buffalo), 43

PACIFIC ocean, 11, 38, 51, 94
Pack-horse men, 158, 161
Pack-horses, 93, 155, 157, 224, 228, 231, 237, 244, 248, 280, 303
Pack-trains, 153, 157-61, 166, 175
Packs, 80, 91, 108, 153, 158, 159, 160, 161, 166
Pacolet River, 286
Panther, 160, 203
Paris, Treaty of (1763), 115; Treaty of (1783), 289
Parker, in Carter's Valley, 230
Pascua Florida, 5
Peace, signs of, 23, 42
Peace towns, of the Creeks, 136
Pearls, 19, 20, 24
Pelts. *See* Skins
Pennsylvania, forts in, 174
Pensacola, Florida, 294
Peoria, Lake, 56, 170
Pepper-sauce, given to the Indians for "fire-water," 162
Perico, Indian guide to De Soto, 17

Persimmons, 20, 28, 104
Peru, 12
Petersburg, Virginia, location of Fort Henry, 78
Pierre Albert. *See* Prieber
Pigs. *See* Hogs
Pinckney Treaty (1795), 306
Pine, 102
"Pinta," ship of Columbus, 3
Pioneer homes. *See* Homes, pioneer
Pioneers, 187, 224, 231, 232, 244, 246, 248, 257-58, 303. *See also* Settlements
Pipe of peace, 142. *See also* Calumet
Pittsburgh, Pennsylvania, location of Fort Duquesne, 174
Pizarro, 12
Plots, Cherokee, against Watauga, 273, 277; French, 143; Spanish, 293-94
Plums, 20
Point St. Ignace. *See* St. Ignace, Point
Ponce de León, Juan, 3-6
Port Royal, S. C., 88
Port Royal River, 88
Portages, 41, 53, 56, 63
Porto Rico, 3, 4, 5
'Possum. *See* Opossum
Pottery, Indian, 139
Poultry, 162
Powder. *See* Gunpowder
Powder horn, 205, 226
"Pox take such a master," 88
Prices of trading goods, 157
Prieber, Christian Gottlieb, 126-130
Priests, 5, 12, 16, 37, 38, 48, 58, 108, 111
Proclamation of 1763, 223
"Promised Land," 227
Prospectors, of land, 210, 243
Prudhomme, Pierre, 64-66, 102
Prudhomme Bluffs, 66
Pumpkins, 104

QUALLA, 20
Quebec, 69

RABBIT, 25, 30
Raccoon, 15
Rafts, 28, 58, 66, 160, 161, 180, 185, 301
Rains, John, 214, 248
Rattlesnakes, 160, 203
Raven, The, Cherokee Warrior, 271, 279
Red Shoes, Choctaw chief, 148-149
"Red" towns, of the Creeks, 136
Reedy Creek, 212
Revolutionary War. *See* American Revolution
Rhododendron, 82, 203
Ribbons, 156, 157, 197
Richmond, Virginia, site of Fort Charles, 175-76
Riflemen, western, 238, 264, 272, 281, 285-89, 301
Rifles, 198, 205, 224, 226, 228, 281. *See also* Guns
Roanoke River, 79, 86
Robertson, James, goes land prospecting, 226-27; lost in a storm, 227-28; leads a party to Watauga, 228; 231, 232, 234, 237; on the Cumberland, 247-59; 276, 277
Runners-of-the-woods, 47, 172
Running Water, Indian village, 298; destroyed, 301
Rutherford, Colonel Griffeth leads expedition against the Cherokees, 280

ST. AUGUSTINE, Florida, Ponce de León lands near, 4, Oglethorpe attacks, 181-82
St. Ignace, Point, 40, 54, 78
St. Joseph River, 55, 56, 63
St. Lawrence River, 37, 46, 48, 51, 56, 107, 108, 303
St. Marks Bay, 10

INDEX

St. Simons Island, 181, 182
Salt, 157, 208, 224, 226
Salt licks, 203, 209, 246
San Salvador, Island of, 3
"Santa Maria," ship of Columbus, 3
Sassafras, 102
Sault Sainte-Marie, 54
Saura, Indian village, 82, 85, 91, 92
Saura Indians, 92
Savannah, Georgia, trading paths to and from, 143, 169; Oglethorpe at, 177, 178; British in, 285
Savannah River, 18, 19, 176, 188
Savannah Tom, 132, 133, 134
Scouts, Indian, 93, 112, 196
Sea islands, forts on, 181
Second Chickasaw Bluff. *See* Chickasaw Bluffs
Sehoy, Creek princess, 294
Settlements, English, 75, 79, 80, 88, 117, 153, 155, 158, 175, 177, 181, 204, 207, 210, 212, 214, 218, 220, 223, 231, 233, 237, 243, 263
Settlements, French, 37, 46, 47, 48, 51, 68, 71, 107, 108, 109, 114, 115, 171, 172
Settlements, Spanish, 5, 37, 87, 154, 168
Sevier, John, as Indian fighter, 235-41, 275, 276; against the British, 286, 287, 299; frontier hospitality of, 240
Shawnee Indians, 48, 49, 90, 204, 208, 242, 270
Shawnee Indian village, 208
Sheep, 5
Shelby, Colonel Evan, invades the Chickamauga country, 283-284
Shelby, Isaac, in the Revolution, 286, 287
Shelters, 5, 28, 168, 196, 215
Shenandoah Valley, 94, 236
Sherrill, "Bonnie Kate," 275
Shipbuilding in the wilderness, 8, 52, 53, 57

Shot-pouch, 205
Signals, 15, 118, 159, 181, 195, 238, 251, 255, 272
Silk, 67
Silkworms, 67
Sitteree, Indian village, 82
Skins, 18, 84, 91, 103, 104, 106, 121, 137, 139, 153, 157, 204, 205, 206, 209, 214, 218, 219, 237; bear, 103, 165, 210: beaver, 90, 154, 157, 206, 208: buffalo, 52, 102, 103, 104, 157, 165, 170, 210: deer, 25, 154, 157, 206, 210, 214: elk, 157: fawn, 104: mink, 157: muskrat, 157: otter, 157; panther, 103; raccoon, 157; dressing of, 208; value of, 208
Slave collars, 13, 16, 126, 190
Slaves, Indian, 13, 15-16, 17, 108, 142; white men as, 109, 112, 132
Smallpox, 251, 253
Smith, James, long hunter, 212-214
Smoke signals, used by Indians, 15
Snakes, 131, 134
South Bend, Indiana, early postage at, 56
South Carolina, Gabriel Arthur in, 88; English traders of, 108, 133; Cherokees in, 116, 117; Prieber in, 127; trading paths in, 176-77; against the Indians, 177, 181; builds forts for Indians, 187-92; and the Cherokees during the French and Indian War, 193-99 *passim;* a pioneer family from, 231; frontiers of attacked by Indians, 279; in the Revolution, 285-89. *See also* Charleston
South seas, 39, 40, 48, 49
Spanish claims, 4, 140, 293
Spanish intrigues, 302-7
Spanish settlements. *See* Settlements, Spanish
Spencer, Thomas Sharp, long hunter, 219-22

Sports, Indian, 137, 147, 233. *See also* Ball play; Chunky
Spotswood, Alexander, expedition of, over the Blue Wall, 93-95
Squaws, Indian, 63, 84, 119, 156, 157, 196-97, 298, 301
Squirrels, 203
Starved Rock, on Illinois River, Fort St. Louis built on, 69, 107, 170
State of Franklin. *See* Franklin, State of
Stewart family, on the "Adventure," 251, 253
Storehouses, 118, 139, 156, 162
Strait of Mackinac. *See* Mackinac, Strait of. *See also* Michilimackinac, Straits of
Straits of Michilimackinac. *See* Michilimackinac, Straits of
Strawberries, 104
Stuart, Captain John, 197-99
Stuart, John, hunter, 216, 218, 219
Sulpitians, 45, 46, 47
Superior, Lake, 54
Swamps, 16, 31, 143, 147, 268
Swannanoa Gap, 280
Sycamore Shoals, conference at, 243; western riflemen at, 287
Sycamore Shoals, Treaty of, 235, 264
Sycamore tree, Spencer's home in, 220

"Talks" (conferences with Indians), British, 269; French, 100, 109, 131, 140
"Talks," Indian, 120, 270, 299
Talladega County, Alabama, 20
Tallahassee, Florida, 8, 17
Tallapoosa River, 136, 141, 172
Tallapoosa Town, 129
Talon, Jean, 39, 40
Tampa Bay, Florida, 6, 13
Tea kettles, 157
Tellico River, 189

Tennessee, De Soto in, 20; Cherokees in, 116 ff.; French traders in, 155; English traders in, 155; Fort Assumption, 173; long hunters in, 212 ff.; settlement in after Treaty of Fort Stanwix, 223 ff.; as territory and state, 241; Cumberland settlement in, 246 ff. *See also* Cherokee country; Needham and Arthur expedition; Fort Loudoun (Loudon); Sevier, John; Watauga
Tennessee River, vii, 20, 83, 85, 91, 100, 125, 175, 189, 203, 213, 248, 250, 252, 255, 256, 268, 283, 284, 296, 301, 302
Texas, 11, 71
Thomas, Isaac, trader, 271, 281
Thompson, Colonel, of Virginia, 272
Tobacco, 303
"Tomahawk rights," 212, 223
Tomatley, Cherokee town, 189
Tombigbee River, 110, 112, 113, 172
Tomo-chici, and Oglethorpe, 177
Tomohitans. *See* Cherokee Indians
Tonty, Henri de, 52, 53, 54, 55, 56, 57-58, 59, 61-63, 65, 68, 69, 107, 108, 170
"Tonty of the Iron Hand." *See* Tonty, Henri de
Tories, 285, 286
Town in the Dogwood Thicket. *See* Dogwood Thicket, Town in
Town-houses, Cherokee, 121, 126, 129; Creek, 136, 137. *See also* Council houses
Traders, 41, 78, 93, 100, 128, 153; how they lived, 154-67; pack-trains of, 157-62; Dutch, 49; English, 49, 89, 108, 113, 123, 127, 128, 129, 131, 142, 143, 145, 147, 148, 149, 169, 172, 176, 177, 192, 265; French, 50, 52, 54, 108, 109, 122, 154, 170

INDEX

Trading centers, French, 46, 47, 168, 170, 171
Trading goods, 53, 54, 91, 100, 106, 108, 109, 153, 154, 156, 157, 161, 162
Trading paths, 134, 140, 167, 169, 176, 177
Trading posts, 168-76; English, 106, 155, 175, 176, 177, 303; French, 45, 46, 49, 51, 52, 53, 58, 62, 65, 125, 154, 155, 174, 175, 302
Trappers, 157
Treaties, with the Indians, 49, 95, 178, 223, 233, 235, 237-38, 264
Treaty of Fort Stanwix (1768), 223
Treaty, Pinckney. *See* Pinckney Treaty
Treaty of Paris (1763), 115
Treaty with Great Britain (Treaty of Paris, 1783), 289
Trent, Captain William, 184
Trinkets, vendors of, 153-67. *See also* Trading goods
Tunbridge, white man in the Chickamauga towns, 297-98
Tunica County, Mississippi, 27 n.
Turkeys, 19, 66, 81, 104, 156, 203, 207, 216
Tuscaloosa, province of, Alabama, 21
Tuscarora Indians, 117
Tuskagee, Cherokee town, 283
Tuskigagee Island Town, Chickamauga town, 297

"UGLY yellow French," 109,
"Unacas" (white men), 273
Upper Creek country, 129
Upper Creek Indians. *See* Creek Indians
Upper Creek villages, 136
Upper towns, Cherokee, 117. *See also* Overhill towns
Upper towns, Creek, 136, 142, 143. *See also* Creek Indians

VACA, Cabeza de. *See* Cabeza de Vaca
Vegetables, 84, 119, 121, 139, 156, 163. *See also* names of vegetables, as Beans
Venango. *See* Fort Machault
Venison, 120, 199, 207, 210
Vincennes, Sieur de, 174
Vincennes, 174, 220, 268, 269
Virginia, English exploration westward from, 78 ff.; Cherokees in, 116; danger to from Indians, 134; English traders from, 155; trading paths in, 168-69; French forts in territory of, 174; forts in, 176; Washington sent from to warn French, 183-84; builds fort for Cherokees, 188-89; trouble of with Cherokees, 193-99 *passim*; migration and exploration from, 204, 212-13, 224; Wataugans from, 231-32; lawless men from, 235; John Sevier from, 236-37; Indian attacks on frontiers of, 242, 270, 279; George Rogers Clark from, 265 ff.; expeditions from against Indians, 281; Cornwallis's surrender in, 289; Thomas Jefferson of, 306
Voyageurs, 58, 148

WABASH RIVER, 173
Walker, Dr. Thomas, 212
Walnut Bend, Mississippi, 27
Ward, Nancy, "Beloved Woman," 270-72; rescues Mrs. Bean 279; friend of the whites, 282
War of Jenkins' Ear. *See* Jenkins' Ear, War of
War parties, 139, 235; planned by the Cherokees, 271, 272
"Warrior who ran away in the night" (De Brahm), 192
Washington, George, early interest of in the West, 183; climbs the Blue Wall, 183; at

Washington (*con.*)
　Fort Machault, 174, 183-84; builds Fort Necessity, 186; with General Forbes, 186-87; in the Revolution, 289; attitude of toward the West, 304; mentioned, 306
Watauga settlement, 223-41; 247, 248, 249, 250, 252, 258, 259, 263, 271, 273, 275, 277, 279, 280, 301, 302
Watauga Association, formed, 233; leases land from the Cherokees, 233
Watauga Purchase, 233
Watauga River, vii, 224, 242, 243, 255, 287, 302
Watauga Valley, 226, 227, 231, 237
Watermelons, 104
Westerners, 263, 284, 289, 303, 305
Western waters, Land of, vii, 100, 116, 154, 168, 183, 210, 240, 302. *See also* Westward-flowing waters
Westward-flowing waters, 33, 68, 86, 199, 215. *See also* Western waters
"Whanga," for mending moccasins, 205
"White leader" (McGillivray) 294
"White" towns, of the Creeks, 136

Wiggan, Eleazer, 123
Wildcats, 41, 203
Wilderness post office, 68
Wilderness Trail, 244, 248, 258
Wilkinson, General James, Spanish agent, 305
Williams, trader, sent to warn Watauga, 271
Williamsburg, Virginia, 94, 266
Williamson, Colonel Andrew, leads expedition against the Cherokees, 280
Willows, 64
Wills Creek, 186
Windsor Castle, Cherokees at, 124
Wine, 93
Winnebago, Lake, 41
Wisconsin River, 41
Wolf Hills, Virginia, 235
Wolf King, Creek warrior, 142, 143
Wolves, 162, 203
Wood, Colonel Abraham, 79, 80, 85, 90, 92
Woodsmen, 57, 81, 210, 214, 216

XUALLA, 20

YADKIN RIVER, 82, 85
Yah-Yah-Tustanage. *See* Great Mortar
Yaupon bush, 118

www.ingramcontent.com/pod-product-compliance
Lightning Source LLC
Chambersburg PA
CBHW021117300426
44113CB00006B/180